# INDIAN INSPIRED
# GLUTEN-FREE
# COOKING

## ALAMELU VAIRAVAN &
## MARGARET PFEIFFER MS, RD, CLS

Hippocrene Books, Inc.
New York

For further information, contact:
Hippocrene Books, Inc.
171 Madison Avenue
New York, NY 10016
www.hippocrenebooks.com


*Library of Congress Cataloging-in-Publication Data*

Vairavan, Alamelu.
  Indian-inspired gluten-free cooking / by Alamelu Vairavan and Margaret Pfeiffer.
      pages cm
  ISBN-13: 978-0-7818-1306-8 (pbk.)
  ISBN-10: 0-7818-1306-9 (pbk.)
  1.  Gluten-free diet--Recipes. 2.  Cooking, Indic.  I. Pfeiffer, Margaret.
  II. Title.
  RM237.86.V35 2013
  641.3--dc23
                                        2012051521



Printed in the United States of America.

# DEDICATION

To George Blagowidow, the visionary Publisher of Hippocrene Books,
for giving Alamelu the opportunity to make a positive difference in the culinary world.

# ACKNOWLEDGEMENTS

Margaret joins me in expressing our profound thanks to my husband, Dr. K. Vairavan, for his continuous inspiration, guidance, and help throughout this book project.

My special thanks also go to my daughter, Valli Gupta, and her husband, Dr. Atul Gupta, and my son, Ashok Vairavan, for their love and support. I must make a special mention of Ashok for his constant enthusiasm, creative ideas, and inspiring words of support. His encouragement and special pride in my culinary activities provided me with the extra energy I needed to sustain my efforts and to keep me moving forward.

I have also received considerable encouragement from many friends. I must make special mention of Patricia Marquardt, Maya Sikdar, Sharon Jewell, Kathy Ruiz, and Sreedevi Vinnakota.

An important contributor to the pictures in this book was my friend and food photographer Linda Guminey, who took beautiful pictures of all the foods we prepared for this book in my kitchen. Linda's tireless and enthusiastic work helped us include a beautiful photo for every recipe.

I cannot say enough about Priti Gress, the Editorial Director at Hippocrene Books, whose encouragement, support, and editorial suggestions were invaluable. This book would not have been possible without Priti's help and support throughout the project.

I would be remiss if I did not mention George Blagowidow, the Publisher of Hippocrene Books, for his unquestioned faith in me as an author. His support for this book, and for my three previous cookbooks, has helped me immeasurably in my goal to spread the word about healthful cooking and eating to the public. George is a great publisher who is also a visionary.

I must also acknowledge the great encouragement of the students in my classes and culinary presentations. The positive and inspiring comments I received from them and from many viewers of my TV show, "Healthful Indian Flavors with Alamelu," from all over the U.S. in the last few years provided me with enormous encouragement as I embarked on this new book project with Margaret.

Alamelu Vairavan
Milwaukee, WI
www.curryonwheels.com

# CONTENTS

# FOREWORD
by Kristen H. Reynolds, M.D.

I am pleased to write this foreword for the cookbook *Indian Inspired Gluten-Free Cooking*. It is a delight to see Indian cooking tailored specifically for those who need to avoid gluten.

As a family and integrative physician specializing in nutrition and wellness, I have read, explored, and lectured on the topic of gluten sensitivity and celiac disease, as well as worked with numerous patients who have experienced health benefits through gluten-free living.

Though in the past gluten sensitivity had been a controversial topic for some in the medical community, recent research reported in the American Journal of Gastroenterology* confirms the existence of non-celiac wheat (gluten) sensitivity as a distinct clinical condition, separate from the widely-accepted autoimmune condition of celiac disease, and the classic allergic condition of wheat allergy. Anyone suffering from these conditions risks both immediate and long-term health consequences if exposed to even the tiniest amount of gluten. This is one of a few areas in medicine where strict elimination of the offending food leads to enormous health benefits.

Hippocrates, the father of medicine, once said, "Let food be thy medicine and medicine be thy food." Food is nourishment, though for those needing to avoid gluten, finding safe foods can be challenging. Gluten elimination is much more than simply avoiding bread and pasta, as gluten is hidden in many ingredients. Indian food is one of the healthiest and easiest cuisines for gluten-intolerant individuals, though one still needs to be vigilant. For instance, the commonly-used Indian spice asafoetida usually contains gluten, unless the spice is blended with rice flour instead of wheat flour.

For those of us for whom gluten avoidance is a way of life, it can be difficult to find recipes that both safely avoid gluten and produce reliably delicious results. Five years ago my family discovered that we were gluten intolerant. After eliminating gluten, my twin daughters' eczema cleared, their asthma improved, and we all felt healthier, happier, and more energetic. Since then we have searched for recipes that are both gluten-free and taste great.

I am grateful to Alamelu and Margaret for creating an excellent, easy-to-use gluten-free Indian cookbook, allowing those of us avoiding gluten to delve into the culinary cuisine of India. Whether or not you avoid gluten, you will find the recipes in this book to be delicious and nutritious, just as food should be.

Kristen H. Reynolds, M.D.
Family & Integrative Medicine Physician
Milwaukee, Wisconsin

---

* Carroccio A, Mansueto P, Iacono, G, et al. Non-Celiac Wheat Sensitivity Diagnosed by Double-Blind Placebo-Controlled Challenge: Exploring a New Clinical Entity. Am J Gastroenterol. 24 July 2012; doi:10.1038/ajg.2012.236. [Epub ahead of print]

# PREFACE
## by Alamelu Vairavan

I have been fortunate to be able to promote my passion for healthful cooking through my cookbooks, television series, and other media outlets. The culinary activities that I have most enjoyed, however, have been the classes and other public presentations that I conducted over the past several years. These events have given me the opportunity to interact with people who are eager to learn healthful ways to cook and enjoy foods.

My classes and presentations have been offered through university and hospital outreach programs and in community centers and libraries. Over time I began to notice that many people at these presentations asked if my recipes are gluten-free. The high level of interest in gluten-free foods surprised me. So I decided to discuss the widespread interest in gluten-free cooking with my friend Margaret Pfeiffer, a Registered Dietitian who has sometimes teamed up with me in my presentations. Margaret assured me that most recipes I had presented in my classes and in my previous books lend themselves naturally to gluten-free cooking. The reason, she pointed out, was that the vegetables and rice dishes that I prepared were enhanced with spices and legumes without any wheat, oat, or barley. She also assured me that if we pick the spices and other ingredients carefully, the resulting foods would indeed be totally gluten-free.

I was intrigued by the idea of writing a gluten-free cookbook. My interest only i n c r e a s e d when more and more people who are gluten-intolerant or gluten-sensitive and were bored with bland, traditional gluten-free foods suggested that I write an Indian-inspired gluten-free cookbook.

In order to learn more about the subject, I did research and took a class on gluten-free cooking. To my surprise, I found that the cooking class and the books available in the market were mostly focused on breads and desserts. This discovery made me wonder about main and wholesome meals that are gluten-free. Also, as Margaret points out in a different section of this book, simply avoiding gluten does not necessarily help one enjoy foods that are healthful in other ways.

Margaret shared my sense that there is an unmet need for a cookbook that helps readers prepare flavorful, wholesome, and nutritious meals that are also gluten-free. We decided to write a book that would present aromatic vegetable, rice, and lean meat dishes for people who are gluten sensitive or gluten intolerant. As a culinary instructor, specializing in spices and legumes, I found in Margaret an ideal partner for writing such a cookbook.

We set out to write a cookbook that would include simple, easy-to-follow recipes for wholesome and flavorful gluten-free foods, to enrich the culinary experience of gluten-sensitive people. For user's convenience, we decided to use only those ingredients that were readily available in regular mainstream grocery stores. Since most of the spices are now commonly available, the scope of the recipes in our book is not restricted but is indeed broad.

Priti Gress of Hippocrene Books, who was the editor of my two previous books, was most enthusiastic and encouraging when she heard about our idea for this new cookbook. She too felt that there was a need for a gluten-free cookbook that was inspired by Indian cooking.

Margaret and I developed new recipes for the cookbook, but not all dishes presented in the book can be considered traditional "Indian" foods. As the title, "Indian-Inspired Gluten-free Cooking" suggests, we present recipes that are largely influenced by Indian cuisine.

We show how you can transform cruciferous vegetables like cauliflower, broccoli, Brussels sprouts, cabbage, kale, and radishes into dishes that are very tasty and visually appealing. Vegetables cooked as seasoned stir-fries, and saucy vegetable dishes cooked in lentil sauces will be appealing to children and adults. Readers will discover that vegetable dishes prepared with tomatoes, onions, ginger, and other spices can be tastier than they ever imagined.

We also feature recipes that use lean proteins such as chicken, turkey, shrimp, and fish. It is useful to note that a rice dish, a lean meat, and a vegetable dish can make one complete meal. For those who are vegetarians, a rice dish served with several vegetable dishes will form a wholesome and enjoyable meal. You can also prepare selected dishes from this book, including appetizers and desserts, and serve them as accompaniments to a traditional western meal.

Our goal has been to help users easily prepare gluten-free aromatic foods, uniting the exquisite flavors of Indian cooking with American comfort food and using only commonly available ingredients. At the end of the day, this cookbook is for anyone—not just those who are gluten sensitive or gluten intolerant—because the recipes are a great way to add tasty, healthful options to your table.

Come join us as we explore gluten-free cooking, and enjoy delicious foods that are also nutritious and flavorful!

# FAQ ON GLUTEN-FREE FOODS

## What is gluten?
Gluten is a protein found in grains such as wheat, rye, and barley. Gluten is what forms the elastic structure of dough that allows it to rise and hold its shape. Gluten is a collective generic term for a variety of specific proteins found in grains that are harmful to people with celiac disease and gluten intolerance or gluten sensitivity. The specific proteins found in various grains include giadin which is found in wheat, hordein in barley, and secalin in rye.

## Where is gluten found?
Grains that contain gluten include wheat, barley, and rye (see page 5). Although oats contain the gluten protein avenin, it is tolerated in limited amounts (1 cup a day) by most but not all individuals. However, oats are often cross contaminated with gluten containing grains. So use of oats labeled gluten-free is recommended.

## What is celiac disease?
Celiac disease is one of the most commonly inherited digestive diseases that damage the small intestines. It is a genetically based autoimmune disorder. It can occur at any age and can be triggered by stress, gastrointestinal or viral infection, surgery, or pregnancy.

## Who gets celiac disease?
Celiac disease is ten times more common than previously thought and affects 1 of every 100 Americans. More than 3 million Americans are affected by celiac disease; more than 95 percent of them remain undiagnosed. Blood tests are available to help diagnose the disease. It is a lifelong condition that is not outgrown or cured but can be successfully treated with a gluten-free diet.

## What is gluten intolerance?
There is no specific test to determine gluten sensitivity or intolerance. Some individuals who have been tested and do not have celiac disease or a wheat allergy may be sensitive to gluten. About 1 in 10 individuals in the United States are in this group and respond well to a gluten-free diet. In gluten intolerance the reaction to gluten is delayed or more subtle. Symptoms are often difficult to identify as specific to gluten intolerance. Many of the symptoms are also attributed to other diseases and conditions, frequently leading to a wrong diagnosis. Sometimes an individual with a gluten intolerance will experience symptoms such as brain fog, fatigue, nasal congestion and stuffiness, migraine headaches, achy joints, itchy rashes, depression, or anxiety. Other symptoms that can commonly occur in individuals sensitive to gluten are diarrhea, gas, bloating, and constipation. But even if there are no GI symptoms, individuals sensitive to gluten may harm their intestines,

damaging or destroying villi (the tiny, fingerlike protrusions lining the small intestine) when they eat gluten. The body's immune system responds to gluten with an inflammatory attack on the small intestine that interferes with the absorption of nutrients needed for good health. Malnourishment occurs which leads to a variety of health problems. Following a gluten-free diet eliminates most symptoms. We recommend that you consult your physician and follow their recommendations if you suspect you have gluten intolerance. We would also advise you to work with a registered dietitian knowledgeable in gluten-free diets to prevent nutrient deficiencies such as fiber, iron, zinc, magnesium, calcium, vitamins A, D, E, B6, B12, and folate. Treatments for asthma, autism, multiple sclerosis, rheumatoid arthritis, lupus, and Sjögren's syndrome sometimes include gluten-free diets. It is best to consult your healthcare provider to determine what is appropriate for you.

## Grains that contain gluten:

Atta or chapatti flour
Barley
Bran (miller's bran)
Bulgur
Couscous
Cracked wheat
Cream of wheat
Durum
Einkorn
Emmer
Farina
Faro
Graham
Kamut
Rye
Semolina (wheat rava or suji)
Spelt
Triticale
Wheat
Whole wheat
Wheat germ

## Other foods that may contain gluten (a partial listing):

Asafoetida powder
Curry pastes
Gravies
Imitation seafood
Marinades
Processed meats (hot dogs, sausages, deli meat)
Sauces
Seitan
Vegetarian meat substitutes

## Gluten-free grains:

Amaranth
Buckwheat
Indian Rice Grass (Montina™)
Millet
Polenta
Rice (basamati, white or brown, jasmine, black rice, wild rice)
Sorghum (Juwar or Milo)
Teff

## Other foods that are gluten-free (a partial list):

Chia seeds
Eggs
Flaxseeds
Fruits
Legumes/Dals
Meats
Nuts (plain not seasoned)
Poultry
Seafood, fresh
Seeds
Spices (check ingredients)
Vegetables, fresh (check ingredients on canned and frozen)

## Gluten-free flours and starches:

Arrowroot
Bean flours: garbanzo bean flour (chickpea, faba, fava, garfava, besam, or gram), lentil flour, pea flour
Coconut flour
Cornmeal
Cornstarch
Flax meal
Nuts, finely ground, such as almond meal
Potato starch
Rice flour (brown or white)
Sorghum flour
Soy flour
Tapioca

# GLUTEN-FREE COOKING AND NUTRITION: THE BASICS

Eating well is the ability to blend nutritional science with the art of preparing foods that are pleasing to the senses—so that we eat for both health and pleasure. A gluten-free diet should be much more than a diet that simply avoids foods with gluten. A gluten-free diet requires close attention to nutrition. It is especially important to get vitamins and minerals that can be missing from a typical gluten-free diet.

All too often the focus is on finding gluten-free replacements for baked goods, breads, desserts, or processed snack foods. If a gluten-free diet relies heavily on packaged and processed foods that include artificial colors, additives, unhealthy fats, and sweeteners, our bodies will not get the nutrients they need to heal. The focus should be on nutrient-rich whole foods that are naturally gluten-free. We must recognize that disease-fighting compounds and antioxidants in real foods are the promoters of good health. Vegetables, fruits, proteins such as chicken (preferably free-range and antibiotic-free), wild fish rich in omega-3s, and grass-fed meats, along with healthy fats and oils, are important for optimal health. Nourishing and satisfying, Indian cuisine typically relies on real (whole), minimally-processed gluten-free foods that are cooked with health-promoting spices.

The notion that a gluten-free diet will result in weight loss is a myth. Many gluten-free cakes, desserts, and breads (when prepared with refined gluten-free flours and starches lacking in fiber) are still high in carbohydrates, sugar, and calories. It is important to remember that a non-healthy treat is still non-healthy even when it is gluten-free. Weight loss is best achieved when the diet is loaded up with naturally gluten-free real foods that are as close to their natural and original state as possible, rather than relying on processed package products.

Every recipe in this book was tested and measured by the authors so that an accurate nutritional analysis could be provided for the specified serving size. The Food Processor Software by ESHA Research was used to analyze recipes. Please note that the nutritional analysis does not include any optional ingredients.

We have included the analysis of each recipe to help those individuals who desire that information. While the nutrient content of foods is important we must weave nutritional science into the art of eating well. Several recipes will be combined at each meal so one that is higher in a specific nutrient can be combined with one that is lower to create a balance that is pleasing to the palate and meeting nutritional goals.

## THE KEY COMPONENTS OF HEALTHY EATING

**Fats:** A certain amount of fat in your diet is necessary for good health. We encourage you to avoid extreme low-fat diets, which in fact do little to reduce cholesterol or improve health. Oil is the fat usually used in Indian cooking. The oils are heated and then aromatic spices are added. Since the spices and herbs are added to hot oil, it is recommended that you use oils that have a high smoking point and those that are low in omega-6, such as canola oil, olive oil, or virgin coconut oil.

**Fiber:** It is recommended that we get 20 to 30 grams of fiber daily. Fruits have 2 to 4 grams per medium piece, berries 3 to 8 grams fiber per cup, vegetables have 2 to 5 grams per half cup, legumes (lentils/dals) have 4 to 8 grams per half cup cooked, and nuts have 1 to 3 grams per ounce. Choosing brown rice or quinoa instead of white rice is another way to increase fiber. Adding lentils to vegetables, common in Indian cooking, is an easy way to boost fiber.

**Potassium:** Potassium is a mineral that helps maintain a healthy fluid balance in our body. Adults need 4,700 mg daily. A potassium-rich diet may help to reduce elevated or high blood pressure. Many vegetables, lentils, and fish are rich sources of potassium. You will note that the potassium content of each recipe is listed.

**Sodium:** Processed foods account for most of the salt and sodium Americans consume. Only a small amount of salt that we consume comes from the salt added at the table and in the kitchen, and only small amounts of sodium occur naturally in food. Eating plans that limit sodium and increase vegetables and fruits can help keep blood pressure levels healthy. By using spices, we were able to cut sodium content in half in many recipes and still produce incredible flavors. If you are beginning to reduce sodium in your diet, you will find that for several weeks foods seem to "need" more salt. But if you continue to eat lower sodium, your palate adjusts and the extra salt is no longer desired.

**Vegetables:** Vegetables provide many health benefits. Most vegetables are naturally low in calories. Filling half your plate with vegetables is a good rule of thumb. Eat vegetables that form a rainbow of colors. Each color represents different healing compounds or phytonutrients with antioxidant, detoxifying, and anti-inflammatory properties that help our bodies function better. We create optimal health when we include the full range of colors daily.

## SPICES USED IN GLUTEN-FREE COOKING

Label reading is a must for anyone on a gluten-free diet, and spices are no exception. We chose to use single-ingredient herbs and spices which are inherently gluten-free, although there is potential for cross contamination. McCormick and Penzeys Spices are two companies that state that ALL of their single-ingredient herbs and spices are gluten-free.

When buying combinations of spices, seasoning mixes, all-purpose seasonings, or other brands of herbs and spices, you need to check the ingredient list carefully. Gluten can appear in mixtures as natural flavorings or the general term "spices." At one time many manufacturers put wheat in their mixes to keep them from clumping. As of 2006, however, if they add wheat it must be identified on the label since wheat is one of the eight major allergens required to be listed with the ingredients.

Check with the manufacturer to see if their natural flavorings are gluten-based or made from corn or other safe ingredients. To verify, always call the manufacturer at the phone number listed on the label and ask, as formulas can change.

### WHOLE SPICES

**Bay Leaves:** These long, dried green leaves add a subtle flavor to any dish. Bay leaves have a sweet, woody aroma much like that of cinnamon, and a slightly pungent flavor. Bay leaves are added to warm oil to enhance the flavor of rice and meat dishes and can be removed from a dish before serving.

**Black Mustard Seeds:** Small, round, black seeds. Raw mustard seeds have almost no smell, but on cooking, they impart an earthy, nutty aroma. When mustard seeds are dropped in a small amount of hot oil, they pop and crackle as they impart their distinctive flavor. Black mustard seeds (also known as brown mustard seeds) are available in spice stores, regular grocery stores, or Indian grocery stores. If you can't find black mustard seeds, you may substitute yellow mustard seeds.

**Black Pepper:** Black pepper is known as the "king of all spices." Black peppercorns add tremendous flavor to many dishes. Pepper was valued as much as gold in the thirteenth century. Today pepper is readily available around the world in both whole and ground form, and used in almost every cuisine. With a spicy hot taste and pungent aroma, pepper is known as an appetite stimulant and as a digestive spice.

**Cinnamon Sticks:** The aromatic-reddish brown bark of the cinnamon tree imparts a rich, sweet flavor to foods. Cinnamon sticks are cracked down to small ½-inch slivers of cinnamon to be used in cooking. The taste is warm, sharply sweet, and aromatic. Cinnamon and bay leaf cooked together enhance the flavor of vegetable, meat, and rice dishes. Cinnamon sticks can be removed before serving. Ground cinnamon can also be used instead of cinnamon slivers (about ¼ to ½ teaspoon of ground cinnamon can be used).

**Cumin Seeds:** Cumin is appreciated for both its aroma and medicinal qualities. The small, oblong seeds are brown and resemble caraway seeds. With its peppery flavor, cumin is an essential ingredient in curry powder and garam masala. When cumin seeds are dry-roasted or added to warm oil, they impart a rich aroma that enhances rice or vegetable dishes.

**Fennel Seeds:** Vibrant green fennel seeds are a common and much-used spice in India. The seeds have a warm, sweet, and intense licorice flavor that turns milder on roasting. Fennel seeds are a powerful antioxidant and also have anti-inflammatory qualities.

**Fenugreek Seeds:** These small, hard, oblong seeds are brown in color and slightly bitter. Roasting the seeds subdues the flavor. Though it is an important spice ingredient in curry powder, fenugreek is an optional ingredient in this cookbook.

**Coconut:** The hard-shelled, edible inner flesh is widely used as a garnish for cooked vegetables and as a base for chutneys and sauces. Shredded fresh coconut is available in the freezer section of natural and Indian grocery stores. Unsweetened shredded dried coconut is also available in natural food stores. All-natural coconut water, found inside the coconut shell, has the perfect nutrition for rapid hydration. Best of all, it is also gluten-free. Note that coconut milk is different from coconut water. Coconut milk is creamy milk extracted from coconut that looks like a heavy cream, and is often used in saucy dishes.

**Whole Dried Red Chili Pepper:** Chilies have a strong, sharp aroma and their taste ranges from mild to dynamite. The level of heat is dependent on the amount of "capsaicin" present in the seeds. Chilies are available fresh, dried, powdered, flaked in oil, and in sauce, bottled, or pickled. Chilies are high in vitamins A and C and have more vitamin C per gram than an orange! Chili peppers are capsicums, in the same family as bell peppers and paprika pods. They range in flavor from rich and sweet to fiery hot. "Sanaam," "Arbol," "Dundicut," "Tien Tsin," and "Cascabel" are all dried hot peppers. Any one of the above is used in gluten-free cooking. To sauté in oil with other spices, one whole pepper is added with other spices. Chili-infused oil gives foods a rich, full-bodied flavor. You may remove whole peppers before serving.

## GROUND SPICES

**Black Pepper Cumin Powder:** Combine both whole spices in equal portions and grind to a fine powder. This spice blend is a great salt substitute! Delicious when sprinkled on fried eggs and also in flavored rice and vegetable dishes.

**Cayenne Pepper (Red Pepper Powder):** Cayenne pepper has the power to make any dish fiery hot, but it also has a subtle flavor-enhancing quality. Cayenne mixed with ground cumin adds marvelous flavor to foods. The hotness of the dish can be controlled by the amount of cayenne pepper used.

**Ground Cardamom:** Among the costliest and most-prized of spices, cardamom is known as the "queen of all spices." Cardamom is a pod consisting of an outer shell with little flavor, and tiny inner seeds with intense flavor. Shelled, ground cardamom has an intensely strong flavor and is easy to use. Ground cardamom is used to flavor rice and meat dishes and also in preparation of spiced chai (tea).

**Ground Cloves:** Ground cloves are used for flavoring sauces and stocks. The flavor is intense, so be sure to use sparingly. Perfect for flavored rice dishes.

**Ground Coriander:** Ground coriander is prepared by roasting and grinding the seeds. Seeds of the coriander plant are the spice. Coriander seeds have a light, lemony flavor that combines well with other spices.

**Ground Cumin (Powdered Cumin):** Ground cumin blends well with many spices, such as cayenne pepper or black pepper, to lend distinctive flavor to any dish.

**Garam Masala:** The heart of most North Indian dishes, this is a blending of several dry-roasted and ground spices, such as coriander seeds, cumin seeds, cardamom, black peppercorns, cloves, cinnamon sticks, and bay leaves. "*Masala*" refers to a combination of several spices, and "*garam*" means spice intensity referring to spice richness.

**Curry Powder:** A blend of many spices such as coriander, fenugreek, cumin, black pepper, red chili pepper, and turmeric. Commercial blends of curry powder are readily available in grocery stores. Curry powders are used in chicken, fish, and shrimp dishes. Gluten-free curry powders are available in sweet curry powder (not too spicy) and hot curry powder (more hot pepper and ginger) varieties, so choose according to your taste.

**Ground Turmeric (Turmeric Powder):** Known as Indian gold, ground turmeric is a yellow root-spice that has been dried and powdered. A natural food coloring, it imparts mustard-like flavor and bright yellow color to any dish. Turmeric contains the compound curcumin, and is recognized by many as an antioxidant, anti-cancer, and anti-inflammatory substance. Growing research suggests that turmeric may help prevent arthritis and a host of other diseases including Alzheimer's. Lately turmeric is becoming increasingly popular with scientists and physicians who are embracing the natural benefits it provides.

**Gluten-free Chili Garlic Sauce:** Readily available in grocery stores, chili-garlic sauce adds zest to chicken and fish dishes.

## STORING SPICES

Most spices keep best in tightly-sealed glass bottles or containers. Spices will retain their quality for many months, even for a year or two, provided they are stored in airtight containers. We highly recommend removing spices, powders, and dals from their plastic wraps and storing them in bottles with identifying labels. Spices kept in the kitchen cupboard in jars will retain flavor, aroma, and color. Dals can also be stored in glass or metal containers. There are various size jars available in spice shops and in discount stores. If you purchase spices, rice, and lentils in bulk, you will have more than what you will need for regular use in the kitchen. The remaining amounts can be stored in a dry, airtight container on a cool pantry shelf.

# STAPLES USED IN GLUTEN-FREE COOKING

## RICE

Rice is one of the most versatile of grains, often served plain with saucy dishes or tossed with vegetables, legumes, desserts, and meats. Rice pilafs are beloved in India, China, and the Middle East. In India, rice is a staple comfort food, served in a variety of flavored rice dishes.

Basmati rice is an aromatic, creamy white or hardy brown long-grain rice grown in the Himalayan foothills of India and in California. Basmati rice is a fragrant, high-quality rice and is preferred for making both plain and flavored rice dishes. It has a nutty taste and comes packaged under several brand names. They are available in natural food stores, in regular grocery stores, and in Indian grocery stores. Basmati grains are finer than other types of rice, and they separate beautifully after they are cooked.

Brown rice is more nutritious than polished white rice, supplying more fiber. When cooked, the plump, rounded kernels of short and medium-grain brown rice are soft, moist, and slightly sticky.

Extra-long-grain rice is used in making plain and flavored rice dishes. It is a good all-purpose rice, available in regular grocery stores.

### Cooking Instructions for Rice

- On the Stovetop:

Rinse the rice with cool water. Slowly pour off the water and place rice in a saucepan. Add the indicated amount of water to the pan, cover, and bring to a boil. Reduce heat and simmer for the indicated time. Leave the cover on and do not stir. If rice is too moist, remove the cover and continue cooking over low heat to allow the water to evaporate. Be careful, it burns easily!

- In a Rice Cooker:

To cook any rice, we highly recommend an automatic electric rice cooker. Rice cookers are readily available in department stores and in Indian and Asian markets. Rice cookers come in various sizes, ranging from a small four-cup size to larger sizes. All you have to do is rinse and drain the rice. Add rice to indicated amount of water and turn the cooker on. When rice is cooked, the cooker automatically shuts off. You cook perfect rice every time with a rice cooker!

## QUINOA (Gluten-free) (*pronounced keen-wa*)

Quinoa is hardy and nutritious with a unique texture and taste. Available in regular and natural food stores, it is a gluten-free complete protein source. It is a member of the same food family as spinach, Swiss chard, and beets. Quinoa comes in tan, red, orange, pink, purple, and black varieties.

## Basic Cooking Instructions for Quinoa

To rinse quinoa, use a sieve with a fine enough mesh to trap the tiny seeds. Immerse the sieve in a big bowl of cold water until the seeds are all covered with water. Rub the seeds with your fingers to help remove the saponin. Lift the strainer with the seeds out of the water. Change the water in the bowl. Repeat 2 or 3 times until the water is clear and no foam forms on the surface.

In a saucepan, put one part quinoa and two parts water. Bring to a boil and then reduce the heat to simmer and cover. Cook about 15 minutes or until the germ separates from the seed. The cooked germ looks like a tiny curl and should have a slight resistance when you eat it.

For a nuttier taste, try dry roasting the quinoa in a skillet for about 5 minutes before adding the water and cooking.

## DALS/LENTILS/LEGUMES

Dals (lentils)/legumes are high in protein and fiber and a staple ingredient in many Indian dishes. There are numerous varieties of dals, but in all our recipes in this cookbook, we have used split red lentils (masoor dal), split mung beans (moong dal), or yellow or green split peas.

Split Red Lentils (Masoor Dal): Easily available in regular grocery stores, these orange-red lentils in split form are used in making saucy dishes. Red lentils cook in only 15 to 20 minutes and make tasty soups and vegetable dishes.

Split Mung Beans (Moong Dal): A golden yellow lentil used in split form. This most versatile lentil cooks quickly and is widely used in making vegetarian dishes.

Yellow or Green Split Peas: A familiar kind of legume, readily available in regular grocery stores. Yellow or green split peas have distinctive texture and taste and cook quickly, in about 30 minutes. When yellow split peas are cooked, they look like corn but have a milder flavor. Cooked split peas add texture, color, and flavor to vegetable dishes.

## Cooking Lentils

Lentils are easy to cook. In each recipe we have given easy-to-follow stovetop cooking instructions. All the above lentils will cook in 20 to 30 minutes.

## OILS

It is important to use an oil with a high smoke point. Choose any of the following oils: canola oil, avocado oil, macadamia oil, high oleic safflower oil, olive oil, or virgin coconut oil.

## SALT

Most salt is highly refined and very white. Some sea salts retain the minerals which appear as small, dark, or colored particles. If you have been advised by your healthcare provider to cut back on sodium, then any form of salt should be reduced as the sodium content is the same by weight. Coarse or kosher salt has less sodium per teaspoon because less "fits" in the spoon than finely ground table salt. Reduced sodium salt has a filler added so if you "salt to taste" and add more you can end up with the same amount of sodium. You can adjust the amount of sodium in our recipes to your taste and health needs. With all the other spices in the dishes, most people do not notice the lack of salt.

## TOMATO SAUCE

The amount of sodium varies in tomato sauces but can be as high as 410 mg per ¼ cup. We chose to use a no-salt-added variety and then added about half the amount of salt typically used. This gave a better flavor and more control over the sodium content of the recipes. You can leave the added salt out completely to reduce sodium even further. You can use regular tomato sauce if desired or use fresh, plump ripe tomatoes pureed into a sauce in a blender.

## CILANTRO (also known as coriander when in dried form)

A distinctively aromatic herb of major importance, which may be purchased as leaves, seeds, or ground coriander. Cilantro is used both as a garnish and for making chutney.

## GARLIC

A bulbous herb composed of individual cloves that is an essential ingredient in Indian cooking. Used in most soups, vegetables, and meat dishes to enhance the flavor. Frequently sautéed in hot oil at the outset of a recipe, it infuses the entire dish with a distinctively pleasing flavor. Garlic with ginger makes a delicious combination paste. Great curative powers are attributed to garlic.

## GINGER ROOT

A root spice with a warm, fresh flavor that is used very often in Indian cooking both as a fundamental ingredient and as a garnish. Ginger in combination with garlic is very popular and adds wonderful flavor to any dish. Ginger is available in powdered form, but fresh ginger is highly recommended for its flavor and healthful qualities. Ginger also aids in digestion.

## GREEN CHILI PEPPERS (SERRANO, JALAPENO, THAI CHILIES)

Fresh unripe chilies impart heat to many Indian dishes. There are a wide variety of chili peppers and you may use any of the many types available. Chilies are used in virtually every savory dish in India. Chilies may be used sparingly, however, or omitted altogether depending on your taste. In general, the smaller the chili, the hotter it is. To store, remove stem, place in a plastic bag and refrigerate up to one week or freeze for longer period of time. Fresh chilies are high in potassium and vitamins A and C as well as naturally low in sodium.

## MINT

Fragrant herb with a uniquely fresh flavor and aroma. Used primarily in cooling chutneys and relishes that balance the more spicy dishes.

## ONIONS

Staple ingredient valued for its flavor and medicinal qualities. Onions sautéed in oil with various spices are the foundation of most dishes. Onions also appear raw in yogurt salad and as a garnish for other dishes.

# SPICES AND CHILIES

Spices have intrinsic health benefits. There is growing evidence that because of their antioxidant and anti-inflammatory properties, spices like turmeric have a healing power in treating or preventing many diseases. Spices also add flavor to foods, reducing the need for salt.

Some people may be reluctant to try recipes with spices, fearing that they do not enjoy hot and spicy foods. But rest assured that the recipes in this book do not have to be too spicy or hot. The hotness of a dish comes mostly from chilies or cayenne. You can use chilies and cayenne in small quantities (as we have in our recipes here) in such a way that they do not overwhelm the vegetables, but add subtle flavors and aromas to the dishes. Vegetable and rice dishes come alive when enhanced by spices and herbs. The result can be tasty and aromatic foods that are hard to resist. Broccoli, Brussels sprouts, spinach, cabbage, and lima beans are tasty and appealing when cooked with spices and legumes. You may be amazed how even vegetable haters can be transformed to vegetable lovers when spices and legumes are used in cooking.

## Facts about chilies

Besides giving foods a "kick," chilies have nutritional values. For instance, ounce for ounce, green chili peppers have twice as much vitamin C as an orange and contain more vitamin C than a carrot. Chili peppers increase circulation and can warm you up on a cold day. Studies have shown that chili peppers do not aggravate and may even help those with ulcers and gastrointestinal problems. Eating chili peppers is a good way to curb the appetite and control cravings. The compound "capsaicin" found in the chili pepper is an anti-inflammatory and an antioxidant.

# SHOPPING LIST FOR SPICES AND OTHER BASICS

## Ground Spices:

- ☐ Ground Black Pepper
- ☐ Cayenne Pepper (Ground Dried Red Chili Pepper)
- ☐ Ground Cardamom
- ☐ Ground Cloves
- ☐ Ground Coriander
- ☐ Ground Cumin
- ☐ Garam Masala
- ☐ Curry Powder (sweet or hot)
- ☐ Ground Turmeric

## Whole Spices (Seed Spices)

- ☐ Bay Leaves
- ☐ Black Mustard Seeds
- ☐ Cinnamon Sticks
- ☐ Cumin Seeds
- ☐ Fennel Seeds
- ☐ Fenugreek Seeds

- ☐ Unsweetened Shredded Dried Coconut
- ☐ Whole Dried Red Chili Pepper – "arbol," "cascabel," "dundicut," "sanaam," "tien tsin" (any of the dried red chilies can be used in gluten-free cooking)
- ☐ Gluten-free Chili Garlic Sauce
- ☐ Nuts: almonds, cashews, peanuts, walnuts, pistachios, pinenuts, pecans
- ☐ Rice: white and brown basmati rice, extra-long-grain rice, jasmine rice, black rice
- ☐ Quinoa
- ☐ Polenta
- ☐ Lentils: split red lentils, split mung beans, yellow or green split peas

# GENERAL COOKING TIPS
# FOR OUR RECIPES

1. Relax and enjoy cooking. Precise measurements are not required here! If you add a little more or less than the amount specified in the recipe, you are not going to spoil the preparation. Most cooks in India do not use measuring cups or spoons. If you like a certain spice, such as cumin, you may use more than the quantity indicated in the recipe. Contrarily, if you dislike a particular spice, you may reduce the amount specified in the recipe or omit the ingredient altogether. There are very few absolutely essential spices or seasonings, given the wealth of spices and aromatic ingredients that make up almost every dish.

2. If you don't have a specific spice or other ingredient listed in the recipe, don't be disheartened. It is usually possible to substitute or omit ingredients and still produce a delicious dish, although with a different taste. In a very short time, you will become familiar with the spices and the possible substitutions.

3. Indian food is not always hot and spicy. It is the chili peppers and cayenne pepper that give the "kick" to a dish. We have indicated only minimal amounts of chili peppers and cayenne pepper in our recipes. You may add more or less chilies as you desire. We have noted "(more or less to taste)" after those spices that are hot so you can adjust to your preference.

4. Use plump, ripened, round tomatoes. By adding more tomatoes, you can cut down on the tomato sauce if you prefer. In some recipes, however, tomato sauce enhances the flavor of the vegetable dish and should not be omitted.

5. Unsweetened shredded dried coconut, available in Indian grocery stores, can be substituted for freshly ground coconut. The unsweetened shredded dried coconut can be used as a garnish and also as a base for making chutney. Use of sweetened coconut is not recommended in savory dishes. You may substitute an equal amount of fresh shredded coconut for the unsweetened shredded dried coconut, which is available in the freezer section of large supermarkets and specialty stores.

6. Most cities have Indian grocery stores. It is also possible to mail-order spices (an Internet search should provide you with information about retailers).

7. Leftovers can be refrigerated or frozen with no detriment to flavor or nutritional value. Place leftovers in a microwave safe dish or in a glass container. Just as wine tastes better with age, Indian food often tastes better after a day or two because of the rich blending of spices and seasonings. Most leftovers can be refrigerated for 3 to 5 days or kept frozen for weeks. Just reheat and enjoy.

8. Dals/lentils, such as mung beans, red lentils, and split peas, can be cooked in large quantities and kept frozen in one-cup portions in microwave-safe containers or any covered containers for ready use any time. Defrost, heat, and use as needed. Cooked dals/lentils can be stored frozen for many weeks with no loss of flavor or nutritional value and will keep fresh in the refrigerator for about three days if placed in a covered container.

9. Our recipes are easy to follow. Once you have assembled all of your ingredients, it usually takes only 20 to 30 minutes to prepare a dish, sometimes even less. The more practiced you become in preparing a recipe, the easier it will be.

10. A word about vegetables: Even if you don't like a particular vegetable, you may be surprised at how much its taste is transformed and enhanced when prepared according to the recipes presented in this book. For example, we have won new fans over to Brussels sprouts with our recipes! Allow this book to expand your taste and that of your family to include a variety of nutritious vegetables in your daily diet.

11. You can always chop the vegetables ahead of time and keep them refrigerated in plastic wrap, ready for use.

12. You can also make the entire dinner early in the day and reheat at dinnertime. Advance preparation actually enhances the flavor of the dishes. Before serving, heat and enjoy. If you do not find time to cook on weekdays, cook some foods over the weekend and refrigerate them. During the week you can just heat and serve the foods. You may be surprised how tasty and aromatic the resulting foods will be. Foods cooked with spices have a characteristic similar to wine. Taste can improve with age, with a difference that age is measured in days and not in years as with wine.

13. Regular stainless steel heavy-bottomed saucepans, nonstick pots and pans, and cast-iron skillets can be used for cooking. An electric rice cooker and a blender are useful but not necessary.

14. Combining Indian and western dishes makes for a very interesting and pleasing dining experience. For example, serving grilled chicken or fish with an Indian rice and vegetable dish can be a pleasant change of pace for your family and friends. Please see the suggested menus section (page 242) for fusion meal ideas.

15. Spices are inexpensive, readily available, and have a long shelf life. They can be purchased as needed. If you purchase bulk spices from an Indian store, you just have to take some time to empty the spices from plastic bags into bottles with lids, label the bottles for familiarity, and store them in the kitchen cabinet.

16. In all the recipes we have used only ingredients available in local grocery stores. All the spices used in this cookbook are readily available in local grocery stores, spice houses, and natural food stores. While there is no need to go to the Indian grocery store you may find some items at a substantial discount there. Please see the shopping list for spices and other basics on page 14 for more information.

17. In many recipes, we sauté black mustard seeds with cumin seeds. However, a split skinned lentil called urad dal, available in Indian grocery stores, can be used instead of the cumin seeds for a more authentic tasting dish.

# APPETIZERS

# BLACK BEAN CUTLETS

*These easy and tasty vegetable patties or "burgers" can be served as a main course or as an appetizer. Serve with any desired chutney such as Tomato Onion Chutney (page 57).*

## INGREDIENTS

1 (15-ounce) can black beans, drained and rinsed (divided)

¼ cup sour cream

2 tablespoons fresh lemon juice

¼ teaspoon ground cumin

¼ teaspoon salt (more or less to taste)

¼ teaspoon ground black pepper

1 teaspoon garam masala

¼ teaspoon cayenne pepper (more or less to taste)

½ medium onion, chopped

2 teaspoons oil

½ cup finely chopped bell pepper (green, red, or yellow)

½ cup chopped fresh cilantro

½ cup stone-ground whole-grain cornmeal (gluten-free)

Yield: 10 cutlets
Serving size: 1 cutlet

1. Set aside half of the beans in a bowl. Place the remaining half of the beans, sour cream, lemon juice, cumin, salt, pepper, garam masala, and cayenne pepper in a food processor and process until smooth. Spoon the bean mixture into the bowl with the reserved beans.

2. In a small skillet or pan, sauté onions in oil on medium heat until translucent. Add bell peppers and cook 1 minute longer while stirring.

3. Add cooked onions and peppers to the bowl with the bean mixture. Add cilantro and cornmeal. Stir to blend evenly.

4. Using ¼-cup portions, form into 10 round patties. Brush or spray with oil and brown patties on both sides in pan. Serve with any chutney.

## NUTRITION PER SERVING

| | | |
|---|---|---|
| 60 calories | 5 mg cholesterol | 3 g fiber |
| 1.5 g fat | 150 mg sodium | 3 g protein |
| 0.5 g saturated fat | 11 g carbohydrate | 166 mg potassium |

# CHICKEN TIKKA KEBABS

*These tender pieces of chicken, marinated in a spice blend and broiled, taste great served with Chickpea and Garlic Chutney (page 43).*

## INGREDIENTS

4 boneless, skinless chicken thighs or breasts, patted dry with paper towels

### MARINADE

½ teaspoon cayenne pepper

¼ teaspoon ground cardamom

¼ teaspoon dry fenugreek/methi leaves (optional)

¼ teaspoon curry powder

¼ teaspoon salt (more or less to taste)

1 tablespoon fresh lemon juice

½ tablespoon grated fresh ginger

½ tablespoon minced garlic

2 tablespoons plain low-fat yogurt

### EQUIPMENT

8 (6-inch) wooden skewers, soaked in water for 30 minutes

Yield: 8 kebabs

Serving size: 1 kebab

1. Cut the chicken into bite-size cubes.

2. Whisk the marinade ingredients in a glass bowl. Add the cubed chicken, turning to coat. Cover and marinate for 1 hour in the refrigerator, stirring several times.

3. Preheat broiler to 500°F. Line a baking sheet with foil.

4. Thread chicken cubes onto the soaked wooden skewers, leaving about ¼-inch space between pieces to allow for even cooking.

5. Place the skewers of chicken on the baking sheet. Spray chicken lightly with oil.

6. Broil for 20 to 25 minutes, turning halfway through cooking time.

## NUTRITION PER SERVING

| | | |
|---|---|---|
| 48 calories | 29 mg cholesterol | 0 g fiber |
| 1.5 g fat | 108 mg sodium | 7 g protein |
| 0.4 g saturated fat | 1 g carbohydrate | 97 mg potassium |

# LENTIL CREPES

*These crepes are an excellent gluten-free substitute for bread, and also make a creative sandwich wrap. Spread with any chutney, then roll up and enjoy.*

## INGREDIENTS

½ cup yellow or green split peas

¼ cup split red lentils (masoor dal)

½ cup split mung beans (moong dal)

½ cup long-grain brown rice

2 dried red chili peppers (more or less to taste)

1 teaspoon cumin seeds

1 teaspoon fennel seeds

1½ cups water

½ teaspoon ground turmeric

½ teaspoon salt (more or less to taste)

½ cup minced onion

¼ cup chopped fresh cilantro

Yield: 15 crepes
Serving size: 1 crepe

1. Soak the split peas, red lentils, mung beans, rice, red chili peppers, cumin seeds, and fennel seeds in 3 cups of warm water for 2 hours. Drain and discard water.

2. Place soaked mixture in a blender with 1½ cups of fresh water. Add turmeric, salt, and onion. Blend to a coarse, thick consistency, adding additional water, a tablespoon at a time, if needed. (The batter should be quite thick; you can add more water when cooking crepes if needed.)

3. Add cilantro and blend a few seconds. The mixture is ready for making the crepes.

4. Heat a skillet over medium heat. Brush with ¼ teaspoon oil or spray with cooking spray. Using ¼ cup of batter for each crepe, spread batter in a circular pattern with the back of a spoon as thinly as possible.

5. Cook crepe until the edges look dry. Loosen the edges with a spatula. Turn over and cook until golden brown, about 1 minute longer. Adjust heat as necessary for even browning. Roll or fold crepes and serve hot.

## NUTRITION PER SERVING

| | | |
|---|---|---|
| 90 calories | 0 mg cholesterol | 2 g fiber |
| 1.5 g fat | 80 mg sodium | 5 g protein |
| 0 g saturated fat | 15 g carbohydrate | 54 mg potassium |

# POTATO CUTLETS

*Transform seasoned mashed potatoes into crispy golden brown cutlets.*

## INGREDIENTS

2 medium Russet potatoes, peeled and cubed (2 cups)

½ teaspoon ground turmeric (divided)

1 tablespoon oil

½ teaspoon cumin seeds

½ cup chopped onion

¼ cup chopped tomato

1 fresh green chili pepper, chopped (more or less to taste)

½ tablespoon grated fresh ginger

⅛ teaspoon cayenne pepper (more or less to taste)

¼ teaspoon salt (more or less to taste)

¼ cup minced fresh cilantro

Yield: 14 cutlets
Serving size: 1 cutlet

1. Place potatoes in 2-quart saucepan. Add enough water to cover potatoes. Add ¼ teaspoon turmeric and bring to a boil. Reduce to a simmer and cook about 20 minutes or until potatoes are tender when pierced with a fork. Drain and discard water. Reserve potatoes.

2. Heat oil in a skillet over medium-high heat (the oil should be hot but not smoking). Add cumin seeds and stir until seeds change color from light brown to semi-dark brown.

3. Add onion, tomato, and green chili pepper. Cook for 1 minute while stirring. Add remaining ¼ teaspoon turmeric, ginger, cayenne, and salt. Stir to blend.

4. Add potatoes and mash as they cook over medium heat for 2 to 3 minutes. Add cilantro and mix.

5. Preheat oven to 400°F.

6. Using 1 tablespoon of potato mixture for each, form potato mixture into balls and flatten into round patties. Spray with cooking spray or brush with oil.

7. Place the patties on a baking sheet. Bake each side for 3 to 5 minutes. (If desired, cook in a skillet: Place potato patties in a slightly-oiled, heated skillet and brown on both sides until golden brown.)

## NUTRITION PER SERVING

| | | |
|---|---|---|
| 40 calories | 0 mg cholesterol | 1 g fiber |
| 2 g fat | 45 mg sodium | 1 g protein |
| 0 g saturated fat | 6 g carbohydrate | 118 mg potassium |

# POTATO FRITTERS (BONDAS)

*"Bondas" are seasoned potatoes coated with a crispy chickpea and rice flour batter and fried. For a healthier version of this traditional Indian dish, try baking the fritters instead.*

## INGREDIENTS

### FILLING

Prepare one recipe of Potato Cutlets* (page 27)

### BATTER

1 cup chickpea flour (also called garbanzo bean, gram, or besan flour)

¼ cup rice flour

¼ teaspoon baking soda

½ teaspoon ground turmeric

½ teaspoon cayenne pepper (more or less to taste)

¼ teaspoon salt (more or less to taste)*

¾ to 1 cup warm water (approximately)

Oil for cooking

Yield: 15 fritters
Serving size: 1 fritter

1. Preheat oven to 400°F if baking.

2. Combine chickpea flour, rice flour, baking soda, turmeric, cayenne, and salt. Add ¾ cup warm water to the dry ingredients, adding the rest as needed. Stir until it forms a smooth paste. The batter should be quite thick. Reserve.

3. Using 2 tablespoons of the potato mixture for each fritter, use oiled hands to form into balls. Dip balls into the batter. Cook as desired (*see below*). Serve warm.

**To fry:** Add oil to a deep heavy saucepan to a depth of 2 to 3 inches and heat until it reaches a temperature of 375°F on a deep-frying thermometer. Fry the balls in oil until golden brown. Drain on paper towels.

**To cook on stove top in pancake puff pan:** Brush each section of the heated pan with generous amount of oil. When balls are browned on the bottom, turn and keep turning as needed until browned on all sides, following directions that come with the pan.

**To bake in the oven:** Place the potato balls inside oiled mini muffin pans and bake at 400°F for about 5 minutes. Remove pan and turn balls, bake 5 minutes longer.

Note: To reheat, preheat oven to 350°F and bake for 5 to 7 minutes.

## NUTRITION PER SERVING

| BAKED: | | | DEEP-FRIED: | | |
|---|---|---|---|---|---|
| 60 calories | 1 g protein | 0 mg cholesterol | 100 calories | 1 g protein | 0 mg cholesterol |
| 2 g fat | 8 g carbohydrate | 105 mg sodium* | 7 g fat | 8 g carbohydrate | 105 mg sodium* |
| 0 g saturated fat | 1 g fiber | 140 mg potassium | 0.5 g saturated fat | 1 g fiber | 140 mg potassium |

*For lower sodium version, omit salt when making Potato Cutlet mixture and batter. Sodium is reduced to 27 mg per serving.

# ROASTED VEGETABLE KEBABS

*The slightly sweet flavors of vegetables emerge during the roasting process and combine with aromatic spices to make this a tasty and nutritious appetizer. Serve with Peanut and Coconut Chutney (page 31).*

## INGREDIENTS

1 tablespoon oil

½ teaspoon ground cumin

1 teaspoon curry powder

½ teaspoon smoked paprika or ⅛ teaspoon cayenne pepper (more or less to taste)

¼ teaspoon salt (more or less to taste)

2½ cups vegetables cut into pieces, such as:

½ medium zucchini, cut in half lengthwise, then sliced in half circles

½ medium yellow squash, cut in half lengthwise, then sliced in half circles

1 cup bell pepper cubes (red, green, and/or yellow)

½ cup baby portabella mushrooms, cut in half

### EQUIPMENT

8 (6-inch) wooden skewers, soaked in water for 30 minutes

Yield: 8 kebabs
Serving size: 1 kebab

1. Preheat oven to 425°F.

2. In a plastic resealable bag combine oil, cumin, curry powder, paprika (or cayenne pepper), and salt. Add vegetables, seal and turn bag several times to coat.

3. Place vegetables onto skewers alternating varieties. Place kebabs in a single layer on a heavy-duty rimmed baking sheet. (Dark baking sheets work best to brown vegetables. Do not use a light-colored pan or aluminum foil which prevents vegetables from browning quickly.)

4. Place in oven and roast about 7 minutes. Check to see if they are starting to brown. If not, return to the oven for 3 to 5 more minutes.

5. Turn and bake about 7 minutes longer or until vegetables are cooked as you like them. The time will vary based on your individual oven.

## NUTRITION PER SERVING

| | | |
|---|---|---|
| 25 calories | 0 mg cholesterol | 1 g fiber |
| 2 g fat | 75 mg sodium | 0 g protein |
| 0 g saturated fat | 2 g carbohydrate | 91 mg potassium |

# SALMON TIKKA KEBABS

*These salmon cubes are marinated in spiced yogurt and then broiled to make an enticing appetizer. Serve with Seasoned Apple Relish (page 55).*

## INGREDIENTS

1 pound boneless skinless wild salmon filet

### MARINADE

½ teaspoon cayenne pepper (more or less to taste)

¼ teaspoon ground cardamom

¼ teaspoon curry powder

¼ teaspoon salt (more or less to taste)

1 tablespoon fresh lemon juice

½ tablespoon grated fresh ginger

½ tablespoon minced garlic

2 tablespoons plain low-fat yogurt

### EQUIPMENT

8 (6-inch) wooden skewers, soaked in water for 30 minutes

Yield: 8 kebabs
Serving size: 1 kebab

1. Cut the salmon into bite-size cubes.

2. Whisk the marinade ingredients in a glass bowl. Add the cubed salmon, turning to coat. Cover and marinate for 1 hour in the refrigerator, turning several times.

3. Preheat broiler to 500°F. Line a baking sheet with foil.

4. Thread salmon cubes onto the soaked wooden skewers, leaving about ¼-inch space between pieces to allow for even cooking.

5. Place the skewers of salmon on the baking sheet. Spray salmon lightly with oil.

6. Broil for 12 to 15 minutes, turning halfway through cooking.

## NUTRITION PER SERVING

| | | |
|---|---|---|
| 90 calories | 25 mg cholesterol | 0 g fiber |
| 3.5 g fat | 105 mg sodium | 13 g protein |
| 1 g saturated fat | 1 g carbohydrate | 257 mg potassium |

# SAVORY TUNA

*Serve this delicious tuna as an appetizer with rice crackers or spread on toasted gluten-free bread for a sandwich. Also makes a great main dish.*

## INGREDIENTS

2 tablespoons oil

3 (½-inch each) slivers cinnamon stick

½ teaspoon fennel seeds

½ teaspoon cumin seeds

1 cup diced onions

½ cup finely chopped tomato

1 tablespoon minced garlic

½ teaspoon ground turmeric

2 teaspoons curry powder

½ teaspoon ground cumin

¼ teaspoon salt (more or less to taste)

3 tablespoons no-salt-added tomato sauce

1 (9-ounce) can light tuna,* packed in water or oil, drained

1 (5-ounce) can light tuna,* packed in water or oil, drained

2 tablespoons chopped walnuts (or any nut desired)

2 tablespoons minced fresh cilantro

Yield: 2 cups

Serving size: ½ cup

1. Heat oil in a skillet over medium-high heat (the oil should be hot but not smoking). Add cinnamon slivers, fennel seeds, and cumin seeds; stir about 1 minute until cumin seeds change color from light brown to semi-dark brown.

2. Add onions, tomato, and garlic. Cook for 1 minute. Add turmeric, curry powder, ground cumin, and salt. Mix and cook for 1 minute while stirring. Add tomato sauce.

3. Add both cans of tuna, mix thoroughly, and continue to cook 5 minutes over medium-low heat.

4. Remove from heat and stir in walnuts and cilantro.

## NUTRITION PER SERVING

| | | |
|---|---|---|
| 250 calories | 45 mg cholesterol | 2 g fiber |
| 11 g fat | 600 mg sodium* | 8 g protein |
| 1 g saturated fat | 7 g carbohydrate | 230 mg potassium |

*For a lower sodium option use a no-salt-added variety of canned tuna. Sodium is reduced to 261 mg per serving.

# SPINACH YOGURT DIP

*Seasoned fresh baby spinach in yogurt makes a savory dip for vegetables or rice crackers and the spinach makes a delicious side dish.*

## INGREDIENTS

1 teaspoon oil

1 teaspoon black mustard seeds

½ teaspoon cumin seeds

½ cup chopped onion

¼ fresh green chili pepper, minced (more or less to taste)

1 tablespoon minced garlic

1 tablespoon grated fresh ginger

6-ounce package (4 cups) baby spinach, chopped

1 teaspoon ground cumin

¼ teaspoon salt (more or less to taste)

1 tablespoon grated fresh coconut or unsweetened shredded dried coconut

¾ cup plain low-fat yogurt

Yield: 1½ cups

Serving size: ¼ cup

1. Heat oil in a skillet over medium-high heat (the oil should be hot but not smoking). Add mustard seeds and cumin seeds and stir until mustard seeds start to pop and cumin seeds change color from light brown to semi-dark brown.

2. Add onions, green chili pepper, garlic, and ginger and cook for 1 to 2 minutes while stirring.

3. Add spinach, ground cumin, and salt. Mix well and cook until spinach is slightly wilted. Add coconut and mix well.

   At this point you can serve it as a side vegetable to any meal (**Seasoned Sauteed Spinach**).

4. To make into a dip, place the spinach in a bowl, allowing it to cool. Stir the yogurt into the cooled spinach. Serve dip at room temperature or store in the refrigerator and serve cold.

## NUTRITION PER SERVING

| | | |
|---|---|---|
| 50 calories | 0 mg cholesterol | 2 g fiber |
| 2 g fat | 170 mg sodium | 3 g protein |
| 1 g saturated fat | 7 g carbohydrate | 111 mg potassium |

# STUFFED BABY PORTABELLA MUSHROOMS

*These mushrooms filled with spinach or tuna can be made ahead. Just refrigerate until ready to bake.*

## INGREDIENTS

12 baby portabella or regular white mushrooms

¼ cup Spinach with Lentils and Coconut (page 173) or Savory Tuna (page 35)

1 tablespoon finely minced roasted red bell pepper (from a jar)

Yield: 12 filled mushrooms

Serving size: 1 mushroom

1. Preheat oven to 350°F.

2. Wipe mushrooms with a damp paper towel. Carefully remove stems from mushrooms. Use the small end of a melon ball scoop to fill mushroom caps with spinach or tuna mixture. Top with a few pieces of red bell pepper.

3. Spray filled mushrooms with cooking spray and bake, uncovered, on a baking sheet for 12 to 15 minutes.

### VARIATION:

For extra flavor, you can sprinkle the mushrooms with Parmesan cheese before baking, if desired.

## NUTRITION PER SERVING

| | | |
|---|---|---|
| 20 calories | 0 mg cholesterol | 0 g fiber |
| 0.5 g fat | 40 mg sodium | 1 g protein |
| 0 g saturated fat | 2 g carbohydrate | 88 mg potassium |

# CHUTNEYS

# CHICKPEA AND GARLIC CHUTNEY

*This chutney can be served as a vegetable dip or as a spread on gluten-free crackers.*

## INGREDIENTS

1 cup canned chickpeas, drained and rinsed

3 cloves garlic

½ teaspoon cumin seeds

1 whole dried red chili pepper (more or less to taste)

¼ teaspoon cayenne pepper (more or less to taste)

1 tablespoon grated fresh ginger

2 tablespoons fresh lemon juice

¼ teaspoon salt (more or less to taste)

½ cup low-fat buttermilk

Yield: 1½ cups
Serving size: ¼ cup

1. Place all ingredients in a blender or food processor; blend or process until a smooth thick consistency.

2. If the mixture is too thick, add additional buttermilk or some water, a tablespoon at a time, to thin to desired consistency.

3. Scrape into a bowl and serve. As an option, garnish with finely chopped red onion and cilantro.

## NUTRITION PER SERVING

| | | |
|---|---|---|
| 60 calories | 0 mg cholesterol | 2 g fiber |
| 0.5 g fat | 130 mg sodium | 3 g protein |
| 0 g saturated fat | 10 g carbohydrate | 158 mg potassium |

# CILANTRO CHUTNEY

*Keep this easy-to-prepare chutney on hand to add an extra dimension of flavor to any sandwich.*

## INGREDIENTS

¼ cup chopped onion

1 tablespoon grated fresh ginger

2 cups coarsely chopped fresh cilantro leaves and stems

1 fresh green chili pepper, chopped (more or less to taste)

16 whole almonds

¼ cup grated fresh coconut or unsweetened shredded dried coconut

½ cup plain yogurt or buttermilk

¼ teaspoon salt (more or less to taste)

½ tablespoon fresh lemon juice

Yield: 1 cup

Serving size: 2 tablespoons

1. Combine onion, ginger, cilantro, chili pepper, almonds, coconut, and plain yogurt or buttermilk in a blender or food processor. Blend or process until a smooth, thick consistency. Thin with additional water to desired consistency.

2. Add salt and lemon juice. Process to blend well. Scrape into a bowl and serve.

## NUTRITION PER SERVING

| | | |
|---|---|---|
| 53 calories | 2 mg cholesterol | 1 g fiber |
| 4 g fat | 81 mg sodium | 1.5 g protein |
| 2.5 g saturated fat | 2 g carbohydrate | 112 mg potassium |

# EGGPLANT CHUTNEY

*Eggplant, tomatoes, and garlic blended with a medley of spices makes a tasty chutney that can be served with gluten-free breads, rice crackers, or raw vegetables.*

### INGREDIENTS

1 tablespoon oil

1 teaspoon black mustard seeds

½ teaspoon cumin seeds

2 cups diced unpeeled fresh eggplant

½ cup chopped tomato

¾ cup chopped onion

1 tablespoon grated fresh ginger

4 cloves garlic, chopped

1 whole dried red chili pepper (more or less to taste)

2 tablespoons no-salt-added tomato sauce

¼ teaspoon ground turmeric

2 teaspoons lemon juice

¼ teaspoon salt (more or less to taste)

1 cup hot water (divided)

¼ cup grated fresh coconut or unsweetened shredded dried coconut

Yield: 2½ cups

Serving size: 2 tablespoons

1. Heat the oil in a skillet over medium heat (the oil should be hot but not smoking). Add mustard seeds and cumin seeds and stir until mustard seeds start to pop and cumin seeds change color from light brown to semi-dark brown.

2. Add eggplant, tomatoes, onions, ginger, and garlic to skillet. Cook and stir for 5 to 7 minutes.

3. Add chili pepper, tomato sauce, turmeric, lemon juice, salt, and ½ cup hot water to the skillet. Cover and cook over medium heat until eggplant softens, about 3 minutes.

4. Transfer to a blender or food processor and add remaining ½ cup hot water and coconut. Blend or process until mixture is a thick, coarse consistency.

5. Scrape into a bowl and serve.

## NUTRITION PER SERVING

| | | |
|---|---|---|
| 20 calories | 0 mg cholesterol | 0 g fiber |
| 1.5 g fat | 30 mg sodium | 0 g protein |
| 0.5 g saturated fat | 2 g carbohydrate | 59 mg potassium |

# MANGO CHUTNEY

*The tartness of unripe mango combined with ginger and chili works well in this chutney.*

## INGREDIENTS

½ cup chopped unripe mango

2 tablespoons grated fresh ginger

1 fresh green chili pepper, chopped (more or less to taste)

2 tablespoons chopped raw cashews

2 tablespoons grated fresh coconut or unsweetened shredded dried coconut

¼ teaspoon cayenne pepper (more or less to taste)

¼ teaspoon salt (more or less to taste)

¼ cup warm water

Yield: 1 cup

Serving size: 2 tablespoons

1. Combine all ingredients in a blender or food processor; blend or process until smooth.

2. If the chutney seems too thick, add additional warm water, 1 tablespoon at a time.

3. Scrape into a dish and serve.

## NUTRITION PER SERVING

| | | |
|---|---|---|
| 30 calories | 1 g protein | 0 mg cholesterol |
| 2 g fat | 4 g carbohydrate | 75 mg sodium |
| 1 g. saturated fat | 1 g fiber | 60 mg potassium |

# MINT CILANTRO CHUTNEY

*The combination of mint and cilantro makes a refreshing chutney. Serve with any savory rice dish or use as a dip with vegetables.*

### INGREDIENTS

2 cups fresh mint leaves (discard stems)

2 cups loosely packed cilantro

½ cup chopped onion

1 or 2 fresh green chili peppers (more or less to taste)

2 tablespoons fresh lemon juice

¼ teaspoon salt (more or less to taste)

½ cup water or plain low-fat yogurt

Yield: 1 cup

Serving size: ¼ cup

1. Combine all ingredients in a blender or food processor; blend or process until smooth.

2. Transfer to a glass container and refrigerator until ready to serve.

## NUTRITION PER SERVING PREPARED WITH WATER

| | | |
|---|---|---|
| 15 calories | 0 mg cholesterol | 1 g fiber |
| 0 g fat | 80 mg sodium | 1 g protein |
| 0 g saturated fat | 3 g carbohydrate | 96 mg potassium |

## NUTRITION PER SERVING PREPARED WITH YOGURT

| | | |
|---|---|---|
| 20 calories | 0 mg cholesterol | 1 g fiber |
| 0 g fat | 90 mg sodium | 1 g protein |
| 0 g saturated fat | 4 g carbohydrate | 131 mg potassium |

# PEANUT AND COCONUT CHUTNEY

*A sure hit when spread on sandwiches, this chutney is also delicious served as a dip with fresh vegetables.*

## INGREDIENTS

1 cup unsalted dry-roasted peanuts

¼ cup grated fresh coconut or unsweetened shredded dried coconut

3 garlic cloves, peeled and cut in half

1 whole dried red chili pepper (more or less to taste)

¼ teaspoon salt (more or less to taste)

¾ to 1 cup warm water

Yield: 1⅓ cups

Serving size: 1 tablespoon

1. Combine all ingredients in a blender or food processor; blend or process until smooth.

2. If the chutney seems too thick, add additional warm water, 1 tablespoon at a time.

3. Scrape into a dish and serve.

## NUTRITION PER SERVING

| | | |
|---|---|---|
| 45 calories | 0 mg cholesterol | 2 g fiber |
| 4 g fat | 30 mg sodium | 3 g protein |
| 1 g saturated fat | 13 g carbohydrate | 233 mg potassium |

# SEASONED APPLE RELISH

*Spread this relish on toasted gluten-free bread for a tasty snack or serve alongside to liven up any fish or chicken dish.*

## INGREDIENTS

2 tablespoons oil

1 teaspoon black mustard seeds

1 Granny Smith apple, shredded

½ teaspoon ground turmeric

¼ teaspoon ground cumin

¼ teaspoon cayenne pepper (more or less to taste)

¼ teaspoon salt (more or less to taste)

Yield: 1 cup

Serving size: ¼ cup

1. Heat oil in a skillet over medium-high heat (the oil should be hot but not smoking). Add mustard seeds and cook and stir until seeds start to pop.

2. Add apple, turmeric, cumin, cayenne pepper, and salt. Cover and cook 2 to 3 minutes.

3. Scrape into a dish and serve warm or cold.

### VARIATION:

To make **Creamy Apple Chutney Dip**, add plain low-fat yogurt. Use an equal measure of yogurt to relish. This can be used as a dip with vegetables.

## NUTRITION PER SERVING

| | | |
|---|---|---|
| 80 calories | 0 mg cholesterol | 1 g fiber |
| 7 g fat | 150 mg sodium | 0 g protein |
| 0.5 g saturated fat | 5 g carbohydrate | 53 mg potassium |

# TOMATO AND ONION CHUTNEY

*This bright, zesty chutney is an excellent staple to keep on hand. It adds instant flavor to a sandwich or works well as a dip for fresh vegetables.*

## INGREDIENTS

1 tablespoon oil

1 whole dried red chili pepper (more or less to taste)

½ teaspoon black mustard seeds

½ cup chopped onion

½ cup chopped tomato

¼ teaspoon ground turmeric

¼ teaspoon ground cumin

¼ teaspoon cayenne pepper (more or less to taste)

¼ teaspoon salt (more or less to taste)

¼ cup plain low-fat yogurt

1 tablespoon minced cilantro

Yield: ½ cup

Serving size: 2 tablespoons

1. Heat oil in a skillet over medium-high heat (the oil should be hot but not smoking). Add chili pepper and mustard seeds and stir 1 to 2 minutes, until mustard seeds start to pop.

2. Add onion and tomato to skillet; cook and stir until onions are translucent.

3. Add turmeric, cumin, cayenne pepper, and salt. Stir for a few minutes until mixture is well-blended. Remove from heat. Cool.

4. Stir in yogurt and cilantro. Serve immediately or chilled.

## VARIATION:

Add ¼ cup shredded carrots along with the onion and tomato in step 2. Add additional yogurt to desired creaminess.

## NUTRITION PER SERVING

| | | |
|---|---|---|
| 60 calories | 0 mg cholesterol | 1 g fiber |
| 4 g fat | 160 mg sodium | 2 g protein |
| 0 g saturated fat | 5 g carbohydrate | 164 mg potassium |

# SOUPS

# BLACK-EYED PEA SOUP

*Fiber-packed black-eyed peas take the lead role in this hearty, satisfying soup.*

## INGREDIENTS

2 tablespoons oil

¼ teaspoon fennel seeds

¼ teaspoon cumin seeds

2 (½-inch each) slivers cinnamon stick

1 bay leaf

½ medium onion, sliced lengthwise

½ cup chopped tomato

3 cups (16 ounces) frozen black-eyed peas

½ teaspoon ground turmeric

½ teaspoon ground cumin

½ teaspoon cayenne pepper (more or less to taste)

½ cup no-salt-added tomato sauce

½ teaspoon salt (more or less to taste)

3 cups water

1 tablespoon minced garlic

2 tablespoons chopped fresh cilantro

Yield: 5 cups

Serving size: 1 cup

1. Heat oil in a 2-quart saucepan over medium heat (the oil should be hot but not smoking). Add fennel seeds, cumin seeds, cinnamon slivers, and bay leaf, and stir until seeds change color from light brown to semi-dark brown.

2. Add onion and tomato. Cook until onion is translucent.

3. Add black-eyed peas, turmeric, cumin, cayenne pepper, tomato sauce, salt, and water. Bring to a boil. Add garlic, reduce to a simmer, cover, and cook about 30 to 45 minutes, until black-eyed peas are tender.

4. Garnish soup with cilantro. Serve warm.

## NUTRITION PER SERVING

| | | |
|---|---|---|
| 210 calories | 0 mg cholesterol | 6 g fiber |
| 7 g fat | 250 mg sodium | 10 g protein |
| 0.5 g saturated fat | 30 g carbohydrate | 616 mg potassium |

# CARROT AND LENTIL SOUP WITH KALE

*Packed with lentils, carrots, kale, and spices, this colorful and fiber-rich vegetarian soup is a meal unto itself.*

## INGREDIENTS

½ medium onion, chopped

½ tablespoon oil

½ pound (2 to 3 medium) carrots, peeled and diced

1 clove garlic, finely chopped

½ tablespoon grated fresh ginger

½ fresh green chili pepper, chopped (more or less to taste; for less "heat" use green bell pepper)

½ cup split red lentils (masoor dal)

2½ cups reduced-sodium vegetable broth

1 cup low-sodium spicy vegetable juice (or water with ¼ teaspoon cayenne pepper, more or less to taste)

½ teaspoon ground turmeric

½ teaspoon ground cumin

1 cup chopped kale leaves, discard stem

1 tablespoon minced fresh cilantro

Yield: 5 cups

Serving size: 1 cup

1. In a 4-quart stockpot over medium heat, sauté the onion in the oil until softened.

2. Add carrots, garlic, ginger, chili pepper, and lentils and sauté for a few minutes.

3. Add broth, vegetable juice (or water and cayenne), turmeric, and cumin. Bring to a boil, then reduce to a simmer, and cook covered for 15 to 20 minutes, until carrots are as tender as you like them.

4. Add kale and cook 3 minutes.

5. Serve garnished with cilantro.

## NUTRITION PER SERVING

| | | |
|---|---|---|
| 130 calories | 0 mg cholesterol | 5 g fiber |
| 2 g fat | 290 mg sodium | 8 g protein |
| 0 g saturated fat | 21 g carbohydrate | 496 mg potassium |

# CAULIFLOWER LENTIL SOUP

*This is a lovely, light aromatic soup. The red lentils add protein and fiber and the delicate spices allow the flavor of the cauliflower to shine through.*

## INGREDIENTS

2 cups water

¼ cup split red lentils (masoor dal)

½ teaspoon ground turmeric (divided)

1½ tablespoons oil

3 (½-inch each) slivers cinnamon stick

1 bay leaf

½ medium onion, sliced lengthwise

½ cup chopped tomato

½ fresh green chili pepper, minced (more or less to taste)

4 cups hot water or vegetable broth

¼ teaspoon ground cardamom

2 teaspoons ground cumin

¼ cup no-salt-added tomato sauce

½ teaspoon salt (more or less to taste)

2 cups cauliflower florets (1-inch pieces)

2 tablespoons minced fresh cilantro

Yield: 5 cups
Serving size: 1 cup

1. Bring 2 cups water to a boil in 1-quart saucepan. Add lentils and ¼ teaspoon turmeric. Reduce heat to medium and cook, uncovered, for about 30 minutes until lentils soften and lose their shape. Do not drain. Reserve.

2. Heat oil in a 3-quart deep saucepan over medium heat (the oil should be hot but not smoking). Add cinnamon slivers and bay leaf and stir a few seconds.

3. Add onion, tomato, green chili pepper, and remaining ¼ teaspoon turmeric. Cook and stir, uncovered, until onions and tomatoes are tender.

4. Add reserved lentils with cooking liquid and hot water or vegetable broth.

5. Add cardamom, cumin, tomato sauce, and salt to saucepan. Stir well. Bring to a boil. Reduce heat. Add cauliflower, cook uncovered about 2 minutes or until cauliflower is just tender. Do not overcook cauliflower.

6. Add cilantro, simmer a few minutes, and serve.

## VARIATION:

Omit cauliflower and increase chopped tomatoes to 1½ cups for **Tomato Lentil Soup.**

## NUTRITION PER SERVING

| | | |
|---|---|---|
| 130 calories | 0 mg cholesterol | 5 g fiber |
| 6 g fat | 320 mg sodium | 5 g protein |
| 0 g saturated fat | 15 g carbohydrate | 383 mg potassium |

# SWEET POTATO QUINOA SOUP

*Quinoa is not a true grain but actually the seeds of a green leafy plant. It is rich in protein and gluten-free. Quinoa, sweet potatoes, corn, and two kinds of beans come together beautifully in this hearty soup.*

## INGREDIENTS

½ cup quinoa

1 medium onion, chopped

2 teaspoons oil

5 cups reduced-sodium vegetable or chicken broth

2 teaspoons ground cumin

½ teaspoon ground turmeric

¼ teaspoon cayenne pepper (more or less to taste)

1 cup frozen cut green beans

¼ cup frozen corn

2 cups peeled and cubed sweet potatoes

1 (15-ounce) can reduced-sodium white beans (cannellini, navy, or chickpeas), drained and rinsed

¼ cup chopped fresh cilantro

Yield: 8 cups

Serving size: 1 cup

1. Rinse quinoa in several changes of water and drain in a fine-mesh strainer. Reserve.

2. In a 3-quart saucepan over medium heat, sauté onion in oil about 3 minutes or until onion is translucent. Add reserved quinoa and stir for a few minutes.

3. Add broth, cumin, turmeric, and cayenne pepper. Bring to a boil, then reduce heat, and simmer for 10 minutes.

4. Add green beans, corn, and sweet potatoes. Bring back to a boil, then reduce heat, cover, and simmer for 5 to 10 minutes, until sweet potatoes are tender.

5. Add white beans and cilantro; heat for 2 minutes and serve.

## NUTRITION PER SERVING

| | | |
|---|---|---|
| 150 calories | 0 mg cholesterol | 7 g fiber |
| 2.5 g fat | 300 mg sodium | 5 g protein |
| 0 g saturated fat | 27 g carbohydrate | 381 mg potassium |

# THIN PEPPERY LEMON SOUP

*Ginger and garlic pair with lemon and chilies in a thin lentil-based soup. It is a perfect way to warm up—and ward away colds—on a chilly day!*

## INGREDIENTS

4 cups water (divided)

¼ cup split red lentils (masoor dal)

½ teaspoon ground turmeric (divided)

1 cup chopped tomato

½ tablespoon grated fresh ginger

½ fresh green chili pepper, chopped (more or less to taste)

1 clove garlic, crushed

½ teaspoon salt (more or less to taste)

¼ teaspoon ground Black Pepper Cumin Powder (page 9)

2 teaspoons fresh lemon juice

2 tablespoons chopped fresh cilantro

Yield: 5 cups

Serving size: 1 cup

1. Bring 2 cups water to a boil in a 2-quart saucepan. Add red lentils and ¼ teaspoon turmeric. Reduce heat to medium and cook, uncovered, for about 20 minutes, until lentils become soft and fall apart. If water evaporates during the cooking process, add another cup.

2. Add the remaining ¼ teaspoon turmeric, tomato, ginger, chili pepper, and garlic and cook over medium-low heat for 2 to 3 minutes.

3. Add remaining 2 cups water, salt, and Black Pepper Cumin Powder. Bring to a boil, then reduce heat and simmer for 3 to 5 minutes.

4. Remove from heat; add lemon juice and cilantro. Stir and serve.

## NUTRITION PER SERVING

| | | |
|---|---|---|
| 45 calories | 0 mg cholesterol | 2 g fiber |
| 0 g fat | 240 mg sodium | 3 g protein |
| 0 g saturated fat | 8 g carbohydrate | 186 mg potassium |

# SALADS

# CARROTS IN SEASONED YOGURT

*Lively spices, ginger, and green chilies give carrots an extra zing in this unique yogurt-based salad!*

## INGREDIENTS

1 teaspoon oil

1 whole dried red chili pepper

¼ teaspoon cumin seeds

½ teaspoon mustard seeds

2 cups peeled and shredded carrots

½ fresh green chili pepper, minced (more or less to taste)

1 tablespoon grated fresh ginger

¼ teaspoon salt (more or less to taste)

½ teaspoon fresh lemon juice

1 cup plain low-fat yogurt

Yield: 1⅔ cups

Serving size: ⅓ cup

1. Heat oil in small skillet over medium heat (the oil should be hot but not smoking). Add red chili pepper, cumin seeds, and mustard seeds; stir until mustard seeds start to pop and cumin seeds change color from light brown to semi-dark brown.

2. Add shredded carrots, green chili pepper, and ginger. Add salt and lemon juice; cook and stir over low heat for a minute or two.

3. Remove from heat. Add yogurt and mix well. Serve warm.

## NUTRITION PER SERVING

| | | |
|---|---|---|
| 60 calories | 5 mg cholesterol | 2 g fiber |
| 2 g fat | 180 mg sodium | 3 g protein |
| 0.5 g saturated fat | 9 g carbohydrate | 178 mg potassium |

# FRUIT AND YOGURT MEDLEY WITH WALNUTS

*Slightly sweet yogurt with a hint of spice surrounds fruit and nuts. This salad makes for a healthful, filling breakfast or afternoon snack.*

## INGREDIENTS

1½ cups plain low-fat yogurt

½ teaspoon sugar (or stevia equivalent)

½ teaspoon ground cumin

⅛ teaspoon cayenne pepper (more or less to taste)

½ cup seedless black grapes, halved

½ cup seedless green grapes, halved

½ firm banana, sliced

1 (5-ounce) can mandarin oranges, drained

¼ cup chopped walnuts

Yield: 2 cups
Serving size: 1 cup

1. Whisk the yogurt, sugar (or stevia), cumin, and cayenne pepper in a bowl until smooth.

2. Add grapes, banana, oranges, and nuts, reserving a few pieces of each. Stir gently.

3. Serve garnished with reserved fruit and nuts.

## NUTRITION PER SERVING

| | | |
|---|---|---|
| 160 calories | 10 mg cholesterol | 2 g fiber |
| 6 g fat | 65 mg sodium | 6 g protein |
| 1.5 g saturated fat | 20 g carbohydrate | 195 mg potassium |

# MINTY CUCUMBER AND YOGURT

*This refreshing salad combines cooling mint, cucumber, and yogurt beautifully and serves as the perfect balance to spicy dishes.*

## INGREDIENTS

½ cup plain low-fat yogurt

½ teaspoon Black Pepper Cumin Powder (page 9)

¼ teaspoon salt (more or less to taste)

½ English cucumber, diced (about 2 cups)

¼ cup minced fresh mint leaves (discard stems)

Yield: 2 cups

Serving size: ½ cup

1. Whisk the yogurt, Black Pepper Cumin Powder, and salt in a bowl until smooth.

2. Mix in cucumber and mint.

3. Serve at room temperature or refrigerate 30 minutes and serve chilled.

## NUTRITION PER SERVING

| | | |
|---|---|---|
| 30 calories | 0 mg cholesterol | 1 g fiber |
| 0.5 g fat | 170 mg sodium | 2 g protein |
| 0 g saturated fat | 4 g carbohydrate | 82 mg potassium |

# POMEGRANATE YOGURT SALAD

*Pomegranates are more popular and readily available than ever these days. Praised for their antioxidant properties, the ruby red gem-like seeds of the pomegranate add crunch and tang to yogurt in this unique salad.*

### INGREDIENTS

½ cup plain low-fat yogurt

¼ teaspoon ground cumin

¼ cup chopped red onion

1 cup pomegranate seeds

1 tablespoon chopped pistachios

Yield: 1 cup

Serving size: ¼ cup

1. Whisk yogurt and cumin until smooth.

2. Stir in onion and pomegranate seeds, reserving a few seeds for garnish.

3. Serve topped with reserved pomegranate seeds and pistachios.

## NUTRITION PER SERVING

| | | |
|---|---|---|
| 50 calories | 0 mg cholesterol | 0.5 g fiber |
| 0.5 g fat | 25 mg sodium | 2 g protein |
| 0 g saturated fat | 10 g carbohydrate | 186 mg potassium |

# POTATO AND POMEGRANATE SALAD

*A new twist on the classic potato salad—this one is enhanced with cucumbers, pomegranate seeds, and spices. Serve on a bed of watercress or baby spinach for added color and crunch.*

## INGREDIENTS

1 cup sliced potatoes (gold, red, and/or purple varieties)

¾ cup pomegranate seeds

½ medium English cucumber, cut into 2-inch lengthwise pieces

½ fresh green chili pepper, finely minced (more or less to taste)

½ teaspoon ground cumin

¼ teaspoon black sesame seeds (optional)

½ teaspoon fresh lemon juice

¼ teaspoon salt (more or less to taste)

Yield: 2 cups
Serving size: ½ cup

1. Place potato slices in a glass bowl with a few tablespoons of water. Microwave for 5 minutes or until tender when pierced with a fork. (Alternatively, boil on stovetop.) Drain and cool.

2. Place pomegranate seeds, cucumber, chili pepper, cumin, sesame seeds (if using), lemon juice, and salt in a bowl and stir. Add potatoes and gently toss to combine.

3. Refrigerate for 1 hour before serving.

## NUTRITION PER SERVING

| | | |
|---|---|---|
| 60 calories | 0 mg cholesterol | 1 g fiber |
| 0 g fat | 150 mg sodium | 2 g protein |
| 0 g saturated fat | 14 g carbohydrate | 76 mg potassium |

# SEASONED VEGETABLE YOGURT SALAD

*This colorful salad is easy to make and the crunch of the vegetables is a nice contrast to the creamy seasoned yogurt.*

### INGREDIENTS

1 cup diced English cucumber

½ cup diced zucchini

½ cup diced yellow summer squash

½ cup diced tomato

1½ cups plain low-fat yogurt

1 teaspoon ground cumin

¼ teaspoon salt (more or less to taste)

Yield: 3 cups

Serving size: ½ cup

1. Place cucumber, zucchini, yellow squash, and tomato in a bowl.

2. In a small bowl, whisk yogurt, cumin, and salt until smooth.

3. Pour yogurt mixture over vegetables. Stir just until coated.

4. Serve immediately or refrigerate and serve chilled.

## NUTRITION PER SERVING

| | | |
|---|---|---|
| 47 calories | 5 mg cholesterol | 1 g fiber |
| 1 g fat | 144 mg sodium | 3 g protein |
| 0.5 g saturated fat | 6 g carbohydrate | 85 mg potassium |

# RICE, QUINOA & POLENTA

# BLACK PEPPER AND CUMIN RICE WITH CASHEWS

*This rice showcases the tasty, aromatic combination of black pepper and cumin. A distinctively savory rice dish, it is excellent served with seafood.*

## INGREDIENTS

1 cup basmati rice

2 cups hot water

2 tablespoons oil

1 whole dried red chili pepper (more or less to taste)

1 teaspoon black mustard seeds

1 cup chopped yellow onion

2 teaspoons Black Pepper Cumin Powder (page 9)

½ teaspoon salt (more or less to taste)

¼ cup dry roasted cashews (or any toasted nut desired)

1 tablespoon finely chopped cilantro

Yield: 3 cups

Serving size: ½ cup

1. Rinse and drain rice. Add rice and 2 cups hot water to a rice cooker, cover, and turn on. When rice cooker turns off, allow rice to cool for a few minutes. Fluff gently to separate the grains. Reserve.

2. Heat oil in a large skillet over medium-high heat (the oil should be hot, but not smoking). Add chili pepper and mustard seeds and stir until mustard seeds start to pop. Add onion and cook for 1 minute while stirring.

3. Add reserved cooked rice, Black Pepper Cumin Powder, and salt and stir until blended. Transfer to a serving bowl and garnish with cashews and cilantro.

## NUTRITION PER SERVING

| | | |
|---|---|---|
| 140 calories | 0 mg cholesterol | 1 g fiber |
| 8 g fat | 200 mg sodium | 2 g protein |
| 1 g saturated fat | 17 g carbohydrate | 81 mg potassium |

# CABBAGE RICE PILAF WITH CASHEWS

*Savory cabbage blended with aromatic basmati rice becomes an easy one-dish meal.*

## INGREDIENTS

½ recipe of Crunchy Cabbage with Ginger and Coconut (page 135)

½ cup brown basmati rice

1½ cups hot water

1 teaspoon oil or butter

¼ cup toasted cashew halves

1 tablespoon finely chopped green onions

Yield: 3½ cups

Serving size: ½ cup

1. Prepare Crunchy Cabbage with Ginger and Coconut; reserve.

2. Rinse and drain rice. Add rice and 1½ cups hot water to a rice cooker, cover, and turn on. When rice cooker turns off, allow rice to cool for a few minutes. Fluff gently to separate the grains.

3. In a skillet, heat oil (or melt butter if using). Add cooked rice and reserved cabbage mixture. Mix together until heated through. Transfer to a serving bowl and garnish with cashews and green onions.

## NUTRITION PER SERVING

| | | |
|---|---|---|
| 117 calories | 1 mg cholesterol | 2 g fiber |
| 6 g fat | 49 mg sodium | 3 g protein |
| 1 g saturated fat | 14 g carbohydrate | 85 mg potassium |

# CARROT RICE PILAF

*This colorful, flavorful pilaf is studded with carrots and nuts and enhanced with a range of enticing spices. A great side dish that goes with everything.*

Yield: 2 cups

Serving size: ½ cup

### INGREDIENTS

½ cup basmati rice

1 cup hot water

2 tablespoons oil

1 bay leaf

3 (½-inch each) slivers cinnamon stick

½ teaspoon cumin seeds

¼ medium onion, sliced lengthwise

½ teaspoon ground cumin

¼ teaspoon salt (more or less to taste)

½ cup shredded carrots

¼ cup toasted pine nuts, cashews, or walnuts

1 tablespoon minced fresh cilantro

¼ cup chopped red onion (optional)

1. Rinse and drain rice. Add rice and hot water to a rice cooker, cover, and turn on. When rice cooker turns off, allow rice to cool for a few minutes. Fluff gently to separate the grains. Reserve rice.

2. Heat oil in a skillet over medium-high heat (the oil should be hot but not smoking). Add bay leaf, cinnamon slivers, and cumin seeds. Stir for a minute until cumin seeds change color from light brown to semi-dark brown.

3. Add onion and cook for 2 minutes while stirring. Add reserved rice, ground cumin, and salt. Cook for a minute while stirring. Add carrots. Fluff rice and carrots gently on low heat.

4. Remove bay leaf and serve garnished with nuts, minced cilantro, and red onion, if using.

## NUTRITION PER SERVING

| | | |
|---|---|---|
| 160 calories | 0 mg cholesterol | 1 g fiber |
| 11 g fat | 160 mg sodium | 2 g protein |
| 1.5 g saturated fat | 15 g carbohydrate | 115 mg potassium |

# CAULIFLOWER RICE PILAF

*Fragrant basmati rice pairs well with cauliflower, peas, and red onion in this dish.*

Yield: 3 cups
Serving size: ½ cup

## INGREDIENTS

½ cup white or brown basmati rice

1 cup hot water

1 tablespoon oil (or ½ tablespoon butter and ½ tablespoon oil)

1 bay leaf

2 (½-inch each) slivers cinnamon stick

¼ teaspoon cumin seeds

½ cup chopped onion

2 cups cauliflower florets

½ teaspoon Black Pepper Cumin Powder (page 9)

½ teaspoon garam masala

¼ teaspoon salt (more or less to taste)

¼ cup frozen green peas, thawed

2 tablespoons toasted cashews, walnuts, or pecans

2 tablespoons chopped red onion

1. Rinse and drain rice. Add rice and hot water to a rice cooker, cover, and turn on. When rice cooker turns off, allow rice to cool for a few minutes. Fluff gently to separate the grains.

2. Add oil (and butter if using) to a skillet and heat over medium heat (the oil should be hot but not smoking). Add bay leaf, cinnamon slivers, and cumin seeds and stir until cumin seeds change color from light brown to semi-dark brown.

3. Add onion and cauliflower and stir-fry for a few minutes. Add Black Pepper Cumin Powder, garam masala, and salt. Add 1 tablespoon water, cover, and cook over medium heat until cauliflower is tender.

4. Stir in cooked basmati rice and peas. Cover and cook over low heat for 1 to 2 minutes.

5. Add nuts and red onion. Stir gently.

## NUTRITION PER SERVING

| | | |
|---|---|---|
| 90 calories | 5 mg cholesterol | 2 g fiber |
| 2.5 g fat | 105 mg sodium | 2 g protein |
| 1 g saturated fat | 15 g carbohydrate | 88 mg potassium |

# CHICKPEA AND APPLE RICE

*Chickpeas and apples are not a combination you see everyday, but they combine delightfully with spices, ginger, chilies, and a hint of coconut in this wholesome, aromatic basmati rice dish.*

## INGREDIENTS

½ cup basmati rice (or brown basmati rice or extra-long-grain enriched rice)

1 cup hot water

1 tablespoon oil

1 whole dried red chili pepper (more or less to taste)

½ teaspoon black mustard seeds

½ cup canned chickpeas, drained and rinsed

¾ cup finely chopped peeled green apple

½ tablespoon grated fresh ginger

1 teaspoon minced fresh green chili pepper (more or less to taste)

1 tablespoon fresh lime juice

½ teaspoon ground turmeric

¼ teaspoon salt (more or less to taste)

1 tablespoon fresh grated coconut or unsweetened shredded dried coconut

¼ cup chopped fresh cilantro or green onions

Yield: 3 cups

Serving size: ½ cup

1. Rinse and drain rice. Add rice and 1 cup hot water to a rice cooker, cover, and turn on. When rice cooker turns off, allow rice to cool for a few minutes. Fluff gently to separate the grains. Reserve.

2. Heat oil in a skillet over medium-high heat (the oil should be hot but not smoking). Add red chili pepper and mustard seeds; stir until mustard seeds start to pop.

3. Add cooked reserved rice, chickpeas, apple, ginger, green chili pepper, lime juice, turmeric, and salt. Mix well and cook over medium-low heat for a minute or two.

4. Stir in coconut and cilantro or green onions.

### VARIATION:

Make **Chickpea and Mango Rice** by using unripe green mangos instead of green apples.

## NUTRITION PER SERVING

| | | |
|---|---|---|
| 80 calories | 0 mg cholesterol | 2 g fiber |
| 3 g fat | 125 mg sodium | 2 g protein |
| 0.5 g saturated fat | 13 g carbohydrate | 85 mg potassium |

# FRAGRANT LEMON RICE

*Enriched with yellow split peas, fragrant ginger, and the tangy taste of lemon, this delicately flavored rice makes a lovely accompaniment to any meal.*

## INGREDIENTS

¼ cup yellow or green split peas

2¼ cups hot water (divided)

1 cup basmati or jasmine rice

¼ cup fresh lemon juice

1 teaspoon salt (more or less to taste)

½ teaspoon ground turmeric

2 tablespoons oil

1 whole dried red chili pepper (more or less to taste)

1 teaspoon black mustard seeds

3 tablespoons grated fresh ginger

1 fresh green chili pepper, finely minced (more or less to taste)

½ teaspoon minced lemon peel

¼ cup roasted unsalted peanuts or pine nuts (optional)

2 tablespoons minced fresh cilantro

Yield: 3½ cups

Serving size: ½ cup

1. Soak split peas in ¼ cup hot water for about 30 minutes. Drain water and reserve.

2. Rinse and drain rice. Add rice and remaining 2 cups hot water to a rice cooker, cover, and turn on. When rice cooker turns off, allow rice to cool for a few minutes. Fluff gently to separate the grains. Reserve.

3. Combine lemon juice, salt, and turmeric; reserve.

4. Heat oil in a skillet over medium-high heat (the oil should be hot but not smoking). Add red chili pepper and mustard seeds and stir until mustard seeds start to pop.

5. Stir in reserved split peas and lemon juice mixture. Reduce heat and simmer, uncovered, for 2 to 3 minutes while stirring.

6. Add ginger, green chili pepper, lemon peel, and cooked reserved rice, stirring gently.

7. Serve garnished with nuts (if desired) and cilantro.

## NUTRITION PER SERVING

| | | |
|---|---|---|
| 140 calories | 0 mg cholesterol | 1 g fiber |
| 7 g fat | 340 mg sodium | 4 g protein |
| 5 g saturated fat | 18 g carbohydrate | 83 mg potassium |

# SPINACH LENTIL RICE

*Colorful and nutritious, this blend of rice and lightly spiced spinach makes a wonderful one-dish meal or side.*

Yield: 3 cups

Serving size: ½ cup

### INGREDIENTS

1 cup cooked Spinach with Lentils and Coconut (page 173)

1½ cups cooked fluffed rice (long-grain white, brown, jasmine, or basmati)

1. Combine spinach mixture and cooked rice in a saucepan.
2. Heat to serving temperature. Garnish with chopped nuts (optional).

## NUTRITION PER SERVING

| | | |
|---|---|---|
| 90 calories | 0 mg cholesterol | 1 g fiber |
| 3.5 g fat | 185 mg sodium | 3 g protein |
| 0.5 g saturated fat | 13 g carbohydrate | 95 mg potassium |

# TOMATO AND GREEN ONION RICE

*A tasty rice dish prepared with a medley of fragrant spices. You can increase the fiber by using brown basmati rice.*

Yield: 4 cups

Serving size: ½ cup

### INGREDIENTS

1 cup brown basmati rice (or white basmati, extra-long-grain, or jasmine)

2 cups hot water

1 tablespoon oil

1 bay leaf

4 (½-inch each) slivers cinnamon stick

½ teaspoon cumin seeds

½ cup onion slices (sliced lengthwise)

1 cup chopped tomato

¼ teaspoon ground turmeric

1 teaspoon garam masala

¼ teaspoon salt (more or less to taste)

¼ cup chopped fresh cilantro

½ cup chopped green onions

¼ cup chopped toasted walnuts or cashews

1. Rinse and drain rice. Add rice and 2 cups hot water to a rice cooker, cover, and turn on. When rice cooker turns off, allow rice to cool for a few minutes. Fluff gently to separate the grains. Reserve.

2. Heat oil in a skillet over medium heat (the oil should be hot but not smoking). Add bay leaf, cinnamon slivers, and cumin seeds. Stir until cumin seeds change color from light brown to semi-dark brown.

3. Add onion and tomato and cook for a few minutes while stirring.

4. Add turmeric, garam masala, salt, and cilantro. Stir well, reduce heat to low, and cook uncovered for 5 minutes.

5. Add reserved cooked rice, green onions, and nuts. Stir gently to combine.

## NUTRITION PER SERVING

| | | |
|---|---|---|
| 90 calories | 0 mg cholesterol | 1 g fiber |
| 4 g fat | 75 mg sodium | 2 g protein |
| 0.5 g saturated fat | 13 g carbohydrate | 98 mg potassium |

# VEGETABLE RICE PILAF

*Lima beans or edamame work nicely in this rice pilaf but you can customize it to your own taste by adding any combination of your favorite mixed vegetables, such as broccoli and kale.*

Yield: 6 cups

Serving size: ½ cup

## INGREDIENTS

1 cup brown or white basmati rice

2 cups hot water

¾ cup frozen lima beans or edamame

½ cup water

1 tablespoon oil

1 bay leaf

¼ teaspoon cumin seeds

¼ teaspoon fennel seeds

½ medium onion, sliced lengthwise

½ cup chopped tomato

¼ cup tomato sauce

¼ teaspoon ground turmeric

1½ teaspoons curry powder

½ teaspoon ground cinnamon

½ teaspoon salt (more or less to taste)

1½ cups coarsely chopped green and yellow bell peppers

¼ cup chopped cashews

¼ cup chopped red onion

1. Rinse and drain rice. Add rice and 2 cups hot water to a rice cooker, cover, and turn on. When rice cooker turns off, allow rice to cool for a few minutes. Fluff gently to separate the grains. Reserve.

2. Cook lima beans or edamame in ½ cup water in a saucepan for 3 to 5 minutes over medium heat until tender. Reserve.

3. Heat oil in a skillet over medium-high heat (the oil should be hot but not smoking). Add bay leaf, cumin seeds, and fennel seeds, and stir until cumin seeds change color from light brown to semi-dark brown.

4. Add onion and tomato and cook for 1 minute while stirring. Add tomato sauce, turmeric, curry powder, cinnamon, and salt. Cook for 3 minutes while stirring.

5. Add bell peppers. Cook for 1 minute. Do not overcook bell peppers.

6. Add reserved cooked rice, reserved lima beans, cashews, and red onion. Cook on low until heated to serving temperature.

## NUTRITION PER SERVING

| | | |
|---|---|---|
| 78 calories | 0 mg cholesterol | 1 g fiber |
| 3 g fat | 156 mg sodium | 2 g protein |
| 1 g saturated fat | 11 g carbohydrate | 156 mg potassium |

# FLAVORED QUINOA

*A nutritional powerhouse, quinoa was called the "mother grain" by the Incas. Technically, quinoa is not a cereal grain like oats or wheat; however the tiny seeds of its plant can be used as a gluten-free substitute for grains. The protein is as complete as that in milk. This spiced quinoa is wonderful on its own or as a side dish to any meal.*

## INGREDIENTS

½ cup quinoa

1 cup hot water

½ teaspoon ground cardamom

⅛ teaspoon ground cinnamon

¼ teaspoon ground coriander

¼ teaspoon ground cumin

½ teaspoon ground turmeric

⅛ teaspoon cayenne pepper (more or less to taste)

⅛ teaspoon salt (more or less to taste)

Yield: 1½ cups

Serving size: ½ cup

1. To rinse quinoa, use a sieve with a fine enough mesh to trap the tiny seeds. Immerse the sieve in a big bowl of cold water until the seeds are covered with water. Rub the seeds with your fingers to help remove the saponin. Lift the strainer with the seeds out of the water. Change the water in the bowl. Repeat 2 or 3 times until the water is clear and no foam forms on the surface.

2. Place rinsed quinoa, hot water, cardamom, cinnamon, coriander, cumin, turmeric, cayenne pepper, and salt in a 2-quart saucepan. Bring to a boil, then reduce heat to simmer and cover. Cook 15 to 20 minutes or until done. (Quinoa is done when the grains become transparent and the spiral-like germ has separated. All of the water should be absorbed.)

3. Fluff gently with a fork several times and serve.

## NUTRITION PER SERVING

| | | |
|---|---|---|
| 110 calories | 0 mg cholesterol | 2 g fiber |
| 2 g fat | 105 mg sodium | 4 g protein |
| 0 g saturated fat | 20 g carbohydrate | 218 mg potassium |

# MUSHROOM AND GREEN PEA QUINOA WITH PISTACHIOS

*Quinoa is a great source of manganese, magnesium, iron, copper, and phosphorous. It comes in a range of colors, the most common being off-white to pale yellow. Try the red or black for an interesting color contrast.*

## INGREDIENTS

1 cup red or white quinoa

2 cups water

1 teaspoon Black Pepper Cumin Powder (page 9)

¼ teaspoon ground cumin

½ teaspoon salt (more or less to taste)

2 tablespoons oil

1 bay leaf

1 teaspoon cumin seeds

½ medium onion, sliced lengthwise

8 ounces mushrooms, sliced (baby portabella, cremini, or white button)

½ cup frozen green peas, thawed

¼ cup pistachios

Yield: 4 cups

Serving size: ½ cup

1. To rinse quinoa, use a sieve with a fine enough mesh to trap the tiny seeds. Immerse the sieve in a big bowl of cold water until the seeds are all covered with water. Rub the seeds with your fingers to help remove the saponin. Lift the strainer with the seeds out of the water. Change the water in the bowl. Repeat 2 or 3 times until the water is clear and no foam forms on the surface.

2. Place rinsed quinoa, 2 cups water, Black Pepper Cumin Powder, ground cumin, and salt in a 2-quart saucepan. Bring to a boil, then reduce heat to simmer and cover. Cook 15 to 20 minutes. Let stand 10 minutes. Fluff gently with a fork.

3. Heat oil in a skillet over medium-high heat (the oil should be hot but not smoking). Add bay leaf and cumin seeds. Stir until cumin seeds change color from light brown to semi-dark brown.

4. Add onion and sauté for a few minutes until translucent. Add mushrooms and sauté over medium-high heat until mushrooms become tender and golden. Remove bay leaf and discard.

5. Add green peas and cooked quinoa, stirring gently to blend. Serve garnished with pistachios.

## NUTRITION PER SERVING

| | | |
|---|---|---|
| 150 calories | 0 mg cholesterol | 2 g fiber |
| 7 g fat | 150 mg sodium | 5 g protein |
| 0.5 g saturated fat | 19 g carbohydrate | 350 mg potassium |

# VEGETABLE QUINOA

*Quinoa contains all nine essential amino acids, making it a complete protein and an excellent nutritional choice. It is rich in lysine, an amino acid that is low in most grains. This easy-to-prepare quinoa features peas and carrots, but you can use any vegetables you have on hand.*

## INGREDIENTS

1 cup red or white quinoa

1 tablespoon oil

1 teaspoon cumin seeds

¼ cup finely chopped onions

¼ teaspoon grated fresh ginger

2½ cups hot water

¼ teaspoon salt (more or less to taste)

½ cup frozen peas and carrots, thawed

¼ cup minced fresh cilantro

2 tablespoons chopped toasted cashews

Yield: 3½ cups

Serving size: ½ cup

1. To rinse quinoa, use a sieve with a fine enough mesh to trap the tiny seeds. Immerse the sieve in a big bowl of cold water until the seeds are all covered with water. Rub the seeds with your fingers to help remove the saponin. Lift the strainer with the seeds out of the water. Change the water in the bowl. Repeat 2 or 3 times until the water is clear and no foam forms on the surface. Reserve.

2. Heat oil in a 2-quart saucepan over medium-high heat (the oil should be hot but not smoking). Add cumin seeds and stir until seeds change color from light brown to semi-dark brown.

3. Add onions and ginger and sauté for a few minutes over medium heat. Add quinoa and cook for 1 minute while stirring. Add 2½ cups hot water and salt; reduce to a simmer. Cover and cook over low heat for about 15 to 20 minutes or until all of the water is absorbed. Add thawed peas and carrots. Fluff with a fork.

4. Add cilantro and cashews; fluff with fork and serve hot.

### VARIATION:

Instead of peas and carrots, use cooked fresh carrots and green beans cut about the same size for even cooking.

## NUTRITION PER SERVING

| | | |
|---|---|---|
| 140 calories | 0 mg cholesterol | 2 g fiber |
| 5 g fat | 100 mg sodium | 4 g protein |
| 1 g saturated fat | 19 g carbohydrate | 230 mg potassium |

# FLAVORFUL POLENTA

*Polenta is made from coarsely ground cornmeal. In this recipe, onions, chilies, ginger, and coconut add incredible flavor to simple polenta. You can eat it on its own or top it with any desired sauce.*

### INGREDIENTS

1 tablespoon oil

½ cup chopped onion

½ fresh green chili pepper, chopped (more or less to taste)

1 tablespoon grated fresh ginger

3 cups hot water

1 teaspoon salt (more or less to taste)

¼ teaspoon cayenne pepper (more or less to taste)

1 teaspoon Black Pepper Cumin Powder (page 9)

1 cup coarse ground cornmeal or polenta

2 tablespoons grated fresh coconut or unsweetened shredded dried coconut

Yield: 3 cups

Serving size: ½ cup or 2 slices

1. Heat oil in a skillet over medium-high heat (the oil should be hot but not smoking). Add onion, chili pepper, and ginger. Cook for 1 minute while stirring.

2. Add 3 cups hot water, salt, cayenne pepper, and Black Pepper Cumin Powder. Bring to a boil. Slowly add polenta, whisking the mixture constantly to avoid lumps (the water should stay at a constant boil). Reduce heat.

3. Switch to a wooden spoon; continue to stir over low heat for 20 minutes. The polenta will thicken and pull away from the sides of the pan. Remove from heat and stir in coconut. Serve immediately or chill to reheat later.

4. To chill and reheat later, transfer cooked polenta into a loaf pan. Smooth the top. Chill for 30 minutes. Turn the pan upside down and let the polenta fall onto a cutting board. It will keep the shape of the pan. Slice into 12 slices, brush with oil and heat in a pan or grill. Serve as a side dish or topped with any of the vegetarian sauce recipes.

### VARIATION:

You may also spread polenta into a 9x13-inch pan. Refrigerate for 15 minutes. Slice, brush with oil, and sauté in a skillet over medium heat until golden.

## NUTRITION PER SERVING

| | | |
|---|---|---|
| 130 calories | 0 mg cholesterol | 2 g fiber |
| 3.5 g fat | 100 mg sodium | 2 g protein |
| 1 g saturated fat | 21 g carbohydrate | 59 mg potassium |

# VEGETABLES

# ASPARAGUS WITH GINGER

*Diagonal cuts of green asparagus contrast beautifully with the red onion in this zesty, colorful vegetable side.*

## INGREDIENTS

1 teaspoon oil

½ teaspoon black mustard seeds

½ teaspoon cumin seeds

¼ cup sliced red onion

½ tablespoon grated fresh ginger

1 pound asparagus, sliced diagonally (about 3 cups)

½ teaspoon ground cumin

⅛ teaspoon salt (more or less to taste)

½ tablespoon grated fresh coconut or unsweetened shredded dried coconut

Yield: 1½ cups

Serving size: ½ cup

1. Heat oil in a skillet over medium-high heat (the oil should be hot but not smoking). Add mustard seeds and cumin seeds and stir until mustard seeds start to pop and cumin seeds change color from light brown to semi-dark brown.

2. Add onion, ginger, and asparagus and cook for 1 minute while stirring.

3. Stir in ground cumin and salt; cover and cook 3 to 5 minutes or until asparagus is tender but still crisp.

4. Add coconut, stir, and serve.

## NUTRITION PER SERVING

| | | |
|---|---|---|
| 70 calories | 0 mg cholesterol | 4 g fiber |
| 2.5 g fat | 105 mg sodium | 4 g protein |
| 0.5 g saturated fat | 8 g carbohydrate | 343 mg potassium |

# BEETS WITH COCONUT

*Vibrant in color and packed with vitamins, beets are one of our favorite vegetables. Here is a unique way to prepare them, enriched with split peas and seasoned with coconut.*

## INGREDIENTS

1 cup water

¼ cup yellow or green split peas or split mung beans (moong dal)

¼ teaspoon ground turmeric

1 pound beets

1 tablespoon oil

½ to 1 dried red chili pepper (more or less to taste)

½ teaspoon mustard seeds

½ teaspoon ground cumin

⅛ teaspoon salt (more or less to taste)

2 tablespoons grated fresh coconut or unsweetened shredded dried coconut

Yield: 2 cups

Serving size: ½ cup

1. Bring 1 cup water to a boil in a saucepan. Add split peas and turmeric. Cook uncovered over medium heat for about 20 minutes or until just tender. Drain and reserve.

2. Steam or boil the beets until tender. When cool enough to handle, peel, quarter, and slice them (you should have about 2 cups).

3. Heat oil in a skillet over medium-high heat (the oil should be hot but not smoking). Add red chili pepper and mustard seeds. Cook about 1 minute or until mustard seeds start to pop.

4. Add sliced beets, cumin, and salt. Stir well. Stir in cooked split peas. Cover and cook on low heat for 2 to 3 minutes.

5. Add coconut and mix gently.

## NUTRITION PER SERVING

| | | |
|---|---|---|
| 100 calories | 0 mg cholesterol | 4 g fiber |
| 5 g fat | 160 mg sodium | 3 g protein |
| 1.5 g saturated fat | 13 g carbohydrate | 383 mg potassium |

# TRI-COLORED BELL PEPPERS

*Crunchy, delicious bell peppers are also rich in vitamin C. This vibrant, colorful side dish is a perfect way to celebrate summer's bounty of bell peppers.*

## INGREDIENTS

1 each red, yellow, and green bell peppers

2 teaspoons oil

1 teaspoon black mustard seeds

½ teaspoon cumin seeds

¼ cup chopped onion

½ teaspoon garam masala

¼ teaspoon ground cumin

⅛ teaspoon salt (more or less to taste)

1 tablespoon grated fresh coconut or unsweetened shredded dried coconut

Yield: 2 cups

Serving size: ½ cup

1. Dice bell peppers into 1-inch cubes, set aside 2 cups mixed.

2. Heat oil in a skillet over medium-high heat (the oil should be hot but not smoking). Add mustard seeds and cumin seeds and stir until mustard seeds start to pop and cumin seeds change color from light brown to semi-dark brown.

3. Add onion and cook for 30 seconds while stirring.

4. Add the 2 cups bell peppers, garam masala, ground cumin, and salt. Cook for 3 minutes or until peppers are crisp yet tender.

5. Add coconut, stir, and serve.

## NUTRITION PER SERVING

| | | |
|---|---|---|
| 60 calories | 0 mg cholesterol | 2 g fiber |
| 3.5 g fat | 78 mg sodium | 1 g protein |
| 1 g saturated fat | 6 g carbohydrate | 193 mg potassium |

# BELL PEPPERS IN LENTIL SAUCE

*This lentil sauce is enhanced with a mixture of colorful peppers and tangy spices. It is wonderful served over rice.*

## INGREDIENTS

2 cups water

¼ cup yellow or green split peas or split mung beans (moong dal)

¼ teaspoon ground turmeric

1 red bell pepper

1 green bell pepper

2 teaspoons oil

1 whole dried red chili pepper (more or less to taste)

1 teaspoon black mustard seeds

½ teaspoon cumin seeds

½ cup chopped onion

1 cup diced fresh tomato

¼ cup no-salt-added tomato sauce

¼ teaspoon cayenne pepper (more or less to taste)

¼ teaspoon salt (more or less to taste)

½ teaspoon fresh lemon juice

¼ cup chopped fresh cilantro

Yield: 3 cups

Serving size: ¾ cup

1. Bring 2 cups water to a boil in 1-quart saucepan. Add split peas or mung beans and turmeric. Reduce heat to medium and cook, uncovered, for about 30 minutes until peas soften. If water evaporates during the cooking process, add ½ cup more. Do not drain. Reserve.

2. Dice bell peppers and reserve 1 cup each.

3. Heat oil in a skillet over medium-high heat (the oil should be hot but not smoking). Add red chili pepper, mustard seeds, and cumin seeds and stir until mustard seeds start to pop and cumin seeds change color from light brown to semi-dark brown.

4. Add onion and tomato and cook 2 to 3 minutes while stirring. Add tomato sauce, cayenne pepper, salt, and lemon juice and cook 2 to 3 minutes while stirring. Add reserved split peas or mung beans and bring to a boil.

5. Add red and green bell peppers. Reduce to low heat, simmer for 2 minutes.

6. Garnish with cilantro and serve.

## NUTRITION PER SERVING

| | | |
|---|---|---|
| 120 calories | 0 mg cholesterol | 3 g fiber |
| 3 g fat | 160 mg sodium | 5 g protein |
| 0 g saturated fat | 19 g carbohydrate | 400 mg potassium |

# GREEN BELL PEPPERS AND RED RADISHES IN LENTIL SAUCE

*If you have never cooked radishes before, you will be pleasantly surprised by how good they are in this preparation. They lose their peppery bite and become much mellower in flavor. Serve this recipe over plain rice or quinoa or as a side dish.*

Yield: 4½ cups

Serving size: 1 cup

## INGREDIENTS

3 cups water

½ cup split red lentils (masoor dal)

1 teaspoon ground turmeric (divided)

2 tablespoons oil

1 whole dried red chili pepper (more or less to taste)

1 teaspoon black mustard seeds

1 teaspoon cumin seeds

½ cup chopped onion

½ cup chopped tomato

1 cup thinly sliced red or Daikon radishes

½ cup no-salt-added tomato sauce

¼ teaspoon ground cumin

1 teaspoon ground coriander

½ teaspoon cayenne pepper (more or less to taste)

¼ teaspoon salt (more or less to taste)

1 cup hot water

1 cup cubed coarsely chopped green bell pepper

¼ cup chopped fresh cilantro

1. Bring 3 cups water to a boil in a 1-quart saucepan. Add lentils and ½ teaspoon turmeric. Reduce heat to medium and cook, uncovered, for about 30 minutes, until lentils soften and lose their shape. If water evaporates during the cooking process, add ½ cup more. Do not drain. Reserve.

2. Heat oil in a skillet over medium-high heat (the oil should be hot but not smoking). Add red chili pepper, mustard seeds, and cumin seeds and stir until mustard seeds start to pop and cumin seeds change color from light brown to semi-dark brown.

3. Add onion, tomato, and remaining ½ teaspoon turmeric and sauté for 1 to 2 minutes. Add radishes and sauté for 1 minute.

4. Stir in tomato sauce, ground cumin, coriander, cayenne pepper, and salt. Cover and cook over medium-low heat, stirring occasionally, for 1 to 2 minutes.

5. Add cooked lentils and 1 cup hot water. Bring to a simmer, cover, and cook about 2 to 5 minutes over medium-low heat, stirring occasionally, until radishes are tender.

6. Add bell pepper and cook about 2 to 3 minutes until just tender.

7. Garnish with cilantro.

## NUTRITION PER SERVING

| | | |
|---|---|---|
| 170 calories | 0 mg cholesterol | 6 g fiber |
| 7 g fat | 150 mg sodium | 7 g protein |
| 0.5 g saturated fat | 21 g carbohydrate | 449 mg potassium |

# BROCCOLI WITH RED ONION AND GINGER

*This savory broccoli stir-fry is rich in flavor and nutrition. It can be paired with rice or makes an excellent side dish to any meal.*

Yield: 3 cups
Serving size: ½ cup

## INGREDIENTS

1 teaspoon oil

½ teaspoon black mustard seeds

½ teaspoon cumin seeds

⅓ cup chopped yellow onion

4 cups chopped broccoli florets and stems (peel tough outer layer from stems first)

1 teaspoon grated fresh ginger

½ fresh green chili pepper, chopped (more or less to taste)

⅛ teaspoon salt (more or less to taste)

½ teaspoon garam masala

1 tablespoon grated fresh coconut or unsweetened shredded dried coconut

⅓ cup chopped red onion

1. Heat oil in a skillet over medium-high heat (the oil should be hot but not smoking). Add mustard seeds and cumin seeds and stir until mustard seeds start to pop and cumin seeds change color from light brown to semi-dark brown.

2. Add yellow onion and cook for 30 seconds while stirring.

3. Add broccoli, ginger, green chili pepper, salt, garam masala, and 1 tablespoon water. Cook covered for 5 minutes or until broccoli is tender but still crisp.

4. Add coconut and red onion, stir and serve.

## NUTRITION PER SERVING

| | | |
|---|---|---|
| 30 calories | 0 mg cholesterol | 2 g fiber |
| 1.5 g fat | 65 mg sodium | 2 g protein |
| 0.5 g saturated fat | 4 g carbohydrate | 177 mg potassium |

# BRUSSELS SPROUTS IN AROMATIC SAUCE

*What could be better than brussels sprouts simmered in an aromatic seasoned sauce?*
*This is delicious served over plain rice or as a side dish.*

## INGREDIENTS

2 tablespoons oil

2 to 4 curry leaves (optional)

1 teaspoon black mustard seeds

½ teaspoon cumin seeds

½ cup chopped onion

½ cup chopped tomato

¼ teaspoon ground turmeric

1 teaspoon cayenne pepper (more or less to taste)

1 teaspoon ground cumin

1 cup no-salt-added tomato sauce

½ teaspoon salt (more or less to taste)

2 cups warm water

1 cup fresh brussels sprouts, cut in half (if large, cut in quarters)

Yield: 2 cups

Serving size: ½ cup

1. Heat oil in a skillet over medium-high heat (the oil should be hot but not smoking). Add mustard seeds and cumin seeds and stir until mustard seeds start to pop and cumin seeds are golden brown.

2. Add onion, tomato, and turmeric and cook for 1 minute.

3. Add cayenne pepper, ground cumin, tomato sauce, and salt. Stir well. Add 2 cups warm water to saucepan. Stir and cook for a few minutes.

4. When the mixture in saucepan begins to boil, add brussels sprouts. Cover and cook over low heat until brussels sprouts are just tender, about 10 minutes. Be careful not to overcook.

## NUTRITION PER SERVING

| | | |
|---|---|---|
| 100 calories | 0 mg cholesterol | 2g fiber |
| 7g fat | 250 mg sodium | 2g protein |
| 0.5g saturated fat | 9g carbohydrate | 400 mg potassium |

# BRUSSELS SPROUTS WITH CHICKPEAS

*Brussels sprouts, chickpeas, and coconut come together in this hearty, fiber rich stir-fry dish.*

## INGREDIENTS

2 cups fresh brussels sprouts

2 tablespoons oil

1 teaspoon black mustard seeds

½ cup chopped onion

½ fresh green chili pepper, chopped (more or less to taste)

1 (16-ounce) can chickpeas, rinsed and drained

¼ teaspoon salt (more or less to taste)

½ teaspoon ground cumin

¼ teaspoon ground turmeric

½ cup grated fresh coconut or unsweetened shredded dried coconut

Yield: 4 cups

Serving size: ½ cup

1. Slice off the stem ends of the brussels sprouts. Cut the sprouts in half lengthwise, then place each half facedown on the cutting board and cut crosswise in strips. Reserve.

2. Heat oil in a skillet over medium-high heat (the oil should be hot but not smoking). Add mustard seeds and stir until mustard seeds start to pop.

3. Add onion and green chili pepper and stir for 30 seconds.

4. Stir in chickpeas, salt, cumin, and turmeric. Cover and cook for a couple of minutes until onion is softened.

5. Add sliced brussels sprouts. Mix well and cook covered for an additional minute or until desired tenderness.

6. Add coconut, stir, and serve.

## NUTRITION PER SERVING

| | | |
|---|---|---|
| 130 calories | 0 mg cholesterol | 4 g fiber |
| 8 g fat | 93 mg sodium | 4 g protein |
| 3 g saturated fat | 13 g carbohydrate | 139 mg potassium |

# ROASTED BRUSSELS SPROUTS

*Roasting is one of our favorite methods for preparing brussels sprouts. The outer leaves crisp and caramelize while roasting, and the results are absolutely delicious.*

## INGREDIENTS

1 tablespoon oil

¼ teaspoon ground cumin

¾ teaspoon garam masala

⅛ teaspoon salt (more or less to taste)

4 cups (1 pound) brussels sprouts, cut in half

Yield: 3 cups

Serving size: ½ cup

1. Preheat oven to 425°F.

2. In a large bowl, combine oil, cumin, garam masala, and salt.

3. Add brussels sprouts and toss until spices and oil are evenly distributed.

4. Place brussels sprouts cut side down in a single layer on a dark, shallow baking sheet. (Do not use a light-colored pan or aluminum foil because they do not allow vegetables to brown as quickly.)

5. Place in oven and roast about 15 minutes. Check if they are starting to brown on bottom. If not, return to oven for 5 more minutes. (Bake until as soft as you like. This will vary based on your individual oven.) Serve immediately.

## NUTRITION PER SERVING

| | | |
|---|---|---|
| 50 calories | 0 mg cholesterol | 3 g fiber |
| 2.5 g fat | 70 mg sodium | 3 g protein |
| 0 g saturated fat | 7 g carbohydrate | 294 mg potassium |

# CABBAGE WITH SEASONED EGGS

*This crunchy protein-rich cabbage side dish is great with rice or as a sandwich or wrap filling. Be sure to prepare all ingredients before you start cooking.*

Yield: 3 cups

Serving size: ½ cup

## INGREDIENTS

1 tablespoon oil

1 teaspoon black mustard seeds

½ teaspoon cumin seeds

¼ cup chopped onion

½ fresh green chili pepper, chopped (more or less to taste)

¼ teaspoon salt (more or less to taste)

4 cups coarsely shredded green cabbage

½ teaspoon cayenne pepper (more or less to taste)

2 eggs

¼ teaspoon ground turmeric

2 tablespoons chopped red onion (optional)

1. Heat oil in a skillet over medium-high heat (the oil should be hot but not smoking). Add mustard seeds and cumin seeds and stir until mustard seeds start to pop and cumin seeds change color from light brown to semi-dark brown.

2. Stir in onion, green chili pepper, and salt. Cover and cook over low heat for 1 minute. Add cabbage and cayenne pepper and cook 1 to 2 minutes, being careful not to overcook cabbage.

3. Whisk eggs with turmeric. Pour egg mixture over cabbage. Stir until the eggs are cooked. Add the red onion (if using) and stir.

## NUTRITION PER SERVING

| | | |
|---|---|---|
| 60 calories | 70 mg cholesterol | 1 g fiber |
| 4 g fat | 180 mg sodium | 3 g protein |
| 0.5 g saturated fat | 4 g carbohydrate | 92 mg potassium |

# CRUNCHY CABBAGE WITH GINGER AND COCONUT

*Cabbage is a favorite in Indian cooking, and Indian seasonings like cumin, ginger, and chilies make this recipe a delicious vegetable option. You can serve this as a warm salad or side dish. It is also delicious when used in Cabbage Rice Pilaf with Cashews (page 89).*

### INGREDIENTS

1 tablespoon oil

1 teaspoon cumin seeds

1 tablespoon yellow or green split peas

4 cups shredded cabbage

1 tablespoon grated fresh ginger

½ fresh green chili pepper, chopped (more or less to taste)

1 teaspoon ground cumin

¼ teaspoon salt (more or less to taste)

1 tablespoon grated fresh coconut or unsweetened shredded dried coconut

Yield: 3 cups

Serving size: ½ cup

1. Heat oil in a skillet over medium-high heat (the oil should be hot but not smoking). Add cumin seeds and split peas and stir until cumin seeds change color from light brown to semi-dark brown.

2. Add cabbage, ginger, and chili pepper. Stir well.

3. Stir in ground cumin and salt. Cover and cook over medium-low heat until cabbage is tender yet crisp.

4. Add the coconut and stir well.

## NUTRITION PER SERVING

| | | |
|---|---|---|
| 50 calories | 0 mg cholesterol | 2 g fiber |
| 3 g fat | 110 mg sodium | 1 g protein |
| 0.5 g saturated fat | 5 g carbohydrate | 106 mg potassium |

# CARROTS AND TOMATOES IN LENTIL SAUCE

*Wholesome lentils, carrots, tomatoes, and seasonings are a lively, flavorful combination in this nutritious sauce.*

## INGREDIENTS

1½ cups water

½ cup split red lentils (masoor dal)

½ teaspoon ground turmeric (divided)

2 tablespoons oil

1 whole dried red chili pepper (more or less to taste)

1 teaspoon black mustard seeds

½ teaspoon cumin seeds

½ cup chopped onion

¼ cup chopped tomato

1 cup peeled and thinly sliced fresh carrots

½ cup no-salt-added tomato sauce

½ teaspoon ground cumin

1 teaspoon ground coriander (optional)

½ teaspoon cayenne pepper (more or less to taste)

¼ teaspoon salt (more or less to taste)

1 cup warm water

¼ cup chopped fresh cilantro

Yield: 4 cups
Serving size: ½ cup

1. Bring 1½ cups water to a boil in a 1-quart sauce-pan. Add lentils and ¼ teaspoon turmeric. Reduce heat to medium and cook, uncovered, for about 30 minutes, until lentils soften and lose their shape. If water evaporates during the cooking process, add another cup. Do not drain. Reserve.

2. Heat oil in a skillet over medium-high heat (the oil should be hot but not smoking). Add red chili pepper, mustard seeds, and cumin seeds and stir until mustard seeds start to pop and cumin seeds change color from light brown to semi-dark brown.

3. Add the onion, tomato, and remaining ¼ teaspoon turmeric and cook for 1 to 2 minutes while stirring.

4. Stir in carrots and cook 1 minute. Stir in tomato sauce, ground cumin, coriander (if using), cayenne pepper, and salt. Cover and cook about 2 to 3 minutes over medium-low heat, stirring occasionally.

5. Add cooked lentils plus 1 cup warm water, and cilantro. Cover and cook over medium-low heat about 5 minutes, stirring occasionally, until carrots are tender.

## NUTRITION PER SERVING

| | | |
|---|---|---|
| 90 calories | 0 mg cholesterol | 3 g fiber |
| 4 g fat | 90 mg sodium | 4 g protein |
| 0 g saturated fat | 11 g carbohydrate | 249 mg potassium |

# CHICKPEAS WITH GINGER AND MANGO

*The tart flavors of unripe mango work so nicely with chickpeas in this variation of a classic Indian dish. This high-protein, high-fiber dish makes a great side or snack. Be sure to prepare all ingredients before you start cooking.*

## INGREDIENTS

1 tablespoon oil

½ teaspoon black mustard seeds

½ teaspoon cumin seeds

1 (15-ounce) can chickpeas, drained and rinsed

1 teaspoon grated fresh ginger

¼ teaspoon ground coriander

¼ teaspoon ground turmeric

¼ teaspoon ground cumin

⅛ teaspoon cayenne pepper (more or less to taste)

¼ teaspoon salt (more or less to taste)

¾ cup chopped fresh unripe mango

1 teaspoon grated fresh coconut or unsweetened shredded dried coconut

Yield: 2 cups

Serving size: ½ cup

1. Heat oil in a skillet over medium-high heat (the oil should be hot but not smoking). Add mustard seeds and cumin seeds, and stir until mustard seeds start to pop and cumin seeds change color from light brown to semi-dark brown.

2. Add chickpeas, ginger, coriander, turmeric, ground cumin, cayenne pepper, and salt. Mix well.

3. Stir in mango, then cover and cook over medium-low heat for 1 to 2 minutes.

4. Add coconut and stir and serve.

### VARIATION:

Substitute unpeeled, diced green apple for mango to make **Chickpeas with Ginger and Apple**.

## NUTRITION PER SERVING

| | | |
|---|---|---|
| 140 calories | 0 mg cholesterol | 5 g fiber |
| 6 g fat | 180 mg sodium | 5 g protein |
| 0.5 g saturated fat | 19 g carbohydrate | 62 mg potassium |

# SEASONED CORN

*Brighten up the flavor of corn with a combination of spices. This corn recipe works perfectly as a side dish as well as a zesty topping on tacos or salads.*

## INGREDIENTS

1 tablespoon oil

1 whole dried red chili pepper (more or less to taste)

½ teaspoon cumin seeds

3 cups fresh or frozen corn kernels

1 teaspoon ground cumin

⅛ teaspoon salt (more or less to taste)

¼ cup finely chopped red onion

1 tablespoon grated fresh coconut or unsweetened shredded dried coconut

Yield: 3 cups

Serving size: ½ cup

1. Heat oil in a skillet over medium-high heat (the oil should be hot but not smoking). Add red chili pepper and cumin seeds, stirring until cumin seeds change color from light brown to semi-dark brown.

2. Add corn, ground cumin, and salt. Stir to blend and cook for a few minutes.

3. Add red onion and coconut. Stir and serve.

## NUTRITION PER SERVING

| | | |
|---|---|---|
| 130 calories | 0 mg cholesterol | 3 g fiber |
| 4.5 g fat | 70 mg sodium | 2 g protein |
| 0.5 g saturated fat | 20 g carbohydrate | 24 mg potassium |

# EGGPLANT CURRY WITH GREEN PEAS

*This delicious eggplant curry can be served as a side dish with Lentil Crepes (page 25), gluten-free breads, or rice.*

## INGREDIENTS

1 eggplant (about 2 pounds)

1 tablespoon oil

½ teaspoon cumin seeds

1 cup finely chopped onion

½ cup finely chopped tomato

1 tablespoon finely minced garlic

1 tablespoon grated fresh ginger

3 tablespoons no-salt-added tomato sauce

½ teaspoon ground turmeric

½ teaspoon ground coriander

½ teaspoon ground cumin

¼ teaspoon garam masala

¼ teaspoon cayenne pepper (more or less to taste)

¼ teaspoon salt (more or less to taste)

½ cup frozen peas, thawed

2 tablespoons minced fresh cilantro

Yield: 2 cups

Serving size: ¼ cup

1. Rub eggplant with some oil. Prick eggplant with fork. Bake at 400°F for 30 to 40 minutes. Let cool. Peel and discard skin; mash the pulp and reserve (about 1½ cups). (Alternate preparation: You can also prepare the eggplant by steaming instead of baking. Cut eggplant in cubes and place in a pot fitted with a collapsible vegetable steamer; steam until fork tender, let cool, then remove skin; mash the pulp and reserve.)

2. Heat 1 tablespoon oil in a skillet over medium-high heat (the oil should be hot but not smoking). Add cumin seeds and stir until seeds change color from light brown to semi-dark brown.

3. Add onion, tomato, garlic, and ginger. Stir and cook for 1 to 2 minutes.

4. Add tomato sauce, turmeric, coriander, ground cumin, garam masala, cayenne pepper, and salt. Cook for 2 to 3 minutes while stirring.

5. Add mashed eggplant and peas and stir. Cover and cook for 3 to 5 minutes.

6. Garnish with cilantro. Serve warm.

## NUTRITION PER SERVING

| | | |
|---|---|---|
| 70 calories | 0 mg cholesterol | 3 g fiber |
| 4 g fat | 105 mg sodium | 2 g protein |
| 0 g saturated fat | 8 g carbohydrate | 239 mg potassium |

# GREEN BEANS WITH CARROTS

*Green beans and sweet carrots combine with classic Indian spices in this vibrant, colorful stir-fry. This dish works nicely with rice or as a vegetable side.*

## INGREDIENTS

1 pound fresh green beans

⅓ pound (2 to 3 medium) fresh carrots, peeled

2 tablespoons oil

1 whole dried red chili pepper (more or less to taste)

1 teaspoon black mustard seeds

½ teaspoon cumin seeds

1 teaspoon grated fresh ginger

1 fresh green chili pepper, minced (more or less to taste)

½ teaspoon ground cumin

¼ teaspoon salt (more or less to taste)

1 tablespoon water

2 tablespoons grated fresh coconut or unsweetened shredded dried coconut

Yield: 4 cups
Serving size: ½ cup

1. Dice beans and carrots into ½-inch pieces and reserve (you should have about 2 cups of each).

2. Heat oil in a skillet over medium-high heat (the oil should be hot but not smoking). Add red chili pepper, black mustard seeds, and cumin seeds and stir until mustard seeds pop and cumin seeds change color from light brown to semi-dark brown.

3. Add diced green beans and carrots and stir well.

4. Stir in ginger, green chili pepper, ground cumin, and salt. Add 1 tablespoon water, cover, and cook on low heat until vegetables are tender but still crisp.

5. Add coconut, stir, and serve.

## NUTRITION PER SERVING

| | | |
|---|---|---|
| 60 calories | 0 mg cholesterol | 2 g fiber |
| 1 g fat | 95 mg sodium | 1 g protein |
| 0 g saturated fat | 6 g carbohydrate | 200 mg potassium |

# GREEN BEANS WITH LENTILS AND COCONUT

*This colorful green and gold dish not only makes a beautiful presentation, but packs a lot of flavor and nutrition as well.*

Yield: 4 cups

Serving size: ½ cup

## INGREDIENTS

1½ pounds fresh green beans

3 cups water

½ cup lentils (split mung beans or yellow or green split peas)

¼ teaspoon ground turmeric

1 tablespoon oil

1 whole dried red pepper

2 to 3 curry leaves (optional)

½ teaspoon black mustard seeds

½ teaspoon cumin seeds

½ cup chopped onion

2 teaspoons grated fresh ginger

¼ teaspoon minced fresh green chili pepper (more or less to taste)

½ teaspoon salt (more or less to taste)

2 tablespoons grated fresh coconut or unsweetened shredded dried coconut

1. Dice green beans into ½-inch pieces (you should have 3 cups). Reserve.

2. Bring 3 cups of water to a boil in a saucepan. Add lentils and turmeric. Reduce heat to medium, cook uncovered for 15 to 20 minutes or until lentils are tender. If water evaporates during the cooking process, add another cup. Drain and reserve.

3. Heat oil in a skillet over medium-high heat (the oil should be hot but not smoking). Add whole dried red pepper, curry leaves (if using), mustard seeds, and cumin seeds and stir until mustard seeds start to pop and cumin seeds change color from light brown to semi-dark brown.

4. Add onion and cook for 2 to 3 minutes while stirring.

5. Add diced green beans, ginger, chili pepper, and salt and stir. Add 1 to 2 tablespoons water, cover and cook for 5 to 7 minutes or until beans are tender.

6. Stir in reserved lentils and coconut. Serve warm.

## NUTRITION PER SERVING

| | | |
|---|---|---|
| 80 calories | 0 mg cholesterol | 4 g fiber |
| 3 g fat | 150 mg sodium | 4 g protein |
| 1 g saturated fat | 10 g carbohydrate | 237 mg potassium |

# HEAVENLY LIMA BEANS

*Delicate spices and tomatoes elevate humble lima beans to a sublime side dish. You won't believe how delicious lima beans can be!*

## INGREDIENTS

1 (16-ounce) package frozen baby lima beans (about 2½ cups)

½ teaspoon ground turmeric (divided)

1 cup water

1 tablespoon oil

1 teaspoon black mustard seeds

½ teaspoon cumin seeds

½ cup chopped onion

1 cup chopped tomato

¾ cup no-salt-added tomato sauce

¼ teaspoon cayenne pepper (more or less to taste)

¼ teaspoon ground cinnamon

1 teaspoon ground cumin

½ teaspoon salt (more or less to taste)

2 tablespoons grated fresh coconut or unsweetened shredded dried coconut

Yield: 3 cups

Serving size: ½ cup

1. Place lima beans, ¼ teaspoon turmeric, and 1 cup water in a saucepan. Bring to a boil, reduce heat to simmer, and cook 3 minutes (beans should still be firm). Do not drain. Reserve.

2. Heat oil in a skillet over medium-high heat (the oil should be hot but not smoking). Add mustard seeds and cumin seeds and stir until mustard seeds start to pop and cumin seeds change color from light brown to semi-dark brown.

3. Add onion and tomato and cook 1 to 2 minutes while stirring.

4. Add tomato sauce, cayenne pepper, cinnamon, ground cumin, salt, and remaining ¼ teaspoon turmeric. Stir mixture until it comes to a boil.

5. Add reserved, undrained lima beans and stir well. Cover and cook on medium heat for 2 to 4 minutes until flavors are blended.

6. Add coconut, stir, and serve.

## NUTRITION PER SERVING

| | | |
|---|---|---|
| 160 calories | 0 mg cholesterol | 6 g fiber |
| 3 g fat | 380 mg sodium | 7 g protein |
| 1 g saturated fat | 24 g carbohydrate | 715 mg potassium |

# LIMA BEANS WITH COCONUT

*Here is a quick, easy-to-prepare lima bean stir-fry that can be served as a side dish for lunch or dinner.*

### INGREDIENTS

1 package (10 to 16 ounces) frozen baby lima beans

1 tablespoon oil

1 whole dried red chili pepper

1 teaspoon black mustard seeds

1 teaspoon cumin seeds

½ cup chopped onion

½ teaspoon cayenne pepper (more or less to taste)

½ teaspoon salt (more or less to taste)

2 tablespoons grated fresh coconut or unsweetened shredded dried coconut

Yield: 2 cups
Serving size: ½ cup

1. Cook lima beans in microwave or on stovetop according to package directions. Drain and set aside.

2. Heat oil in a skillet over medium-high heat (the oil should be hot but not smoking). Add red chili pepper, mustard seeds, and cumin seeds and stir until mustard seeds pop and cumin seeds are golden brown.

3. Add onion and cook 1 minute while stirring. Stir in drained lima beans, cayenne pepper, and salt.

4. Add coconut, stir, and serve.

## NUTRITION PER SERVING

| | | |
|---|---|---|
| 173 calories | 0 mg cholesterol | 6 g fiber |
| 7 g fat | 250 mg sodium | 7 g protein |
| 1 g saturated fat | 22 g carbohydrate | 407 mg potassium |

# LENTIL CRUMBLE WITH COCONUT

*This delicious, textured side dish made with split peas is rich in heart-healthy soluble fiber.*

## INGREDIENTS

½ cup yellow or green split peas

2 whole dried red chili peppers (more or less to taste)

1½ teaspoons cumin seeds (divided)

1 teaspoon fennel seeds

¼ cup warm water

3 tablespoons oil

1 teaspoon black mustard seeds

1 cup chopped onion

½ teaspoon ground turmeric

¼ teaspoon cayenne pepper (more or less to taste)

½ teaspoon salt (more or less to taste)

2 tablespoons chopped cilantro

2 tablespoons grated fresh coconut or unsweetened shredded dried coconut

Yield: 2 cups

Serving size: ⅓ cup

1. Place split peas in a bowl and cover with hot water. Let soak for 30 minutes.

2. Drain peas and place in a blender or food processor with red chili peppers, 1 teaspoon cumin seeds, fennel seeds, and ¼ cup warm water. Blend or process until the texture of coarse cornmeal.

3. Pour mixture into a microwave-safe dish, cover with a small plate, and microwave on high for 3 minutes. Mixture will feel somewhat firm. Cool for 5 minutes. Break into small pieces with a fork. Reserve.

4. Heat oil in a skillet over medium-high heat (the oil should be hot but not smoking). Add black mustard seeds and remaining ½ teaspoon cumin seeds and stir until mustard seeds start to pop and cumin seeds change color from light brown to semi-dark brown.

5. Add onion and cook for 30 seconds while stirring.

6. Add reserved crumbled split-pea mixture, turmeric, cayenne pepper, and salt. Continue to cook over medium-low heat for 2 to 4 minutes, while stirring, until the split peas become golden and grainy in texture.

7. Add cilantro and coconut, stir, and serve.

## NUTRITION PER SERVING

| | | |
|---|---|---|
| 130 calories | 0 mg cholesterol | 4 g fiber |
| 9 g fat | 200 mg sodium | 3 g protein |
| 2 g saturated fat | 10 g carbohydrate | 70 mg potassium |

# MUSHROOMS WITH ONION AND GARLIC

*This easy-to-prepare mushroom dish, seasoned with ginger, cumin, and garlic, makes a delicious accompaniment to just about any meal.*

## INGREDIENTS

8 ounces fresh mushrooms (white button, shiitake, cremini, or portabella)

1 tablespoon oil

½ teaspoon cumin seeds

½ medium onion, sliced lengthwise

½ tablespoon grated fresh ginger

4 cloves garlic, minced

½ teaspoon Black Pepper Cumin Powder (page 9)

¼ teaspoon salt (more or less to taste)

2 tablespoons chopped fresh cilantro or red onion

Yield: 2 cups
Serving size: ½ cup

1. Rinse and dry mushrooms thoroughly. Slice and reserve.

2. Heat oil in a skillet over medium-high heat (the oil should be hot but not smoking). Add cumin seeds and stir until seeds change color from light brown to semi-dark brown.

3. Add onion, ginger, and garlic. Cook for 1 minute while stirring.

4. Add mushrooms, Black Pepper Cumin Powder, and salt. Cook for 3 to 5 minutes over medium-high heat while stirring.

5. Add cilantro or red onion and serve warm.

## NUTRITION PER SERVING

| | | |
|---|---|---|
| 70 calories | 0 mg cholesterol | 1 g fiber |
| 3.5 g fat | 150 mg sodium | 2 g protein |
| 0 g saturated fat | 7 g carbohydrate | 316 mg potassium |

# OKRA WITH ONION AND TOMATO

*This lightly seasoned blend of okra and tomato can be served as a side dish or over rice or quinoa. Okra is a good source of soluble fiber.*

## INGREDIENTS

2 tablespoons oil

½ teaspoon black mustard seeds

½ teaspoon cumin seeds

¼ cup chopped onion

¼ cup chopped tomato

½ cup no-salt-added tomato sauce

½ teaspoon ground turmeric

½ teaspoon cayenne pepper (more or less to taste)

½ teaspoon ground cumin

¼ teaspoon salt (more or less to taste)

2 cups fresh okra, sliced (or 2 cups frozen cut okra)

1 tablespoon grated fresh coconut or unsweetened shredded dried coconut

Yield: 2 cups

Serving size: ½ cup

1. Heat oil in a skillet over medium-high heat (the oil should be hot but not smoking). Add mustard seeds and cumin seeds and stir until mustard seeds start to pop and cumin seeds change color from light brown to semi-dark brown.

2. Add onion and tomato. Cook for 1 to 2 minutes while stirring.

3. Add tomato sauce, turmeric, cayenne pepper, ground cumin, and salt. Cook for 1 to 2 minutes while stirring.

4. Add okra and stir to coat with sauce. Cover and cook over medium-low heat for 10 minutes or until okra is tender.

5. Add coconut, stir, and serve.

## NUTRITION PER SERVING

| | | |
|---|---|---|
| 100 calories | 0 mg cholesterol | 3 g fiber |
| 8 g fat | 152 mg sodium | 2 g protein |
| 1 g saturated fat | 8 g carbohydrate | 328 mg potassium |

# POTATO AND VEGETABLE MEDLEY

*You may recognize this as the beloved classic Indian Aloo Gobi (Spiced Cauliflower, Peas, and Potatoes). Serve with rice or quinoa for a meatless main dish.*

## INGREDIENTS

½ pound Yukon Gold potatoes, peeled and cut into ½-inch cubes (about 1 cup)

2 tablespoons oil

½ teaspoon black mustard seeds

½ teaspoon cumin seeds

½ cup chopped onion

1 cup chopped tomato

1 tablespoon minced fresh ginger

1 tablespoon minced garlic

½ teaspoon ground turmeric

½ teaspoon ground coriander

⅛ teaspoon cayenne pepper (more or less to taste)

½ teaspoon garam masala

½ teaspoon ground cumin

¼ teaspoon salt (more or less to taste)

1½ cups cauliflower, cut into small florets, or brussels sprouts, quartered

½ cup frozen green peas, thawed, or cooked lima beans

Yield: 3 cups

Serving size: ½ cup

1. Place cubed potatoes in a glass bowl with a few tablespoons of water. Partially cook for 2 minutes in microwave. (Alternatively, boil for 5 minutes on stovetop.) Reserve.

2. Heat oil in a skillet over medium-high heat (the oil should be hot but not smoking). Add mustard seeds and cumin seeds and stir until mustard seeds start to pop and cumin seeds change color from light brown to semi-dark brown.

3. Add onion, tomato, ginger, and garlic and cook on medium-high heat 2 to 3 minutes while stirring, until onions are translucent.

4. Add turmeric, coriander, cayenne pepper, garam masala, ground cumin, and salt. Stir well.

5. Stir in reserved potatoes. Cover and cook for 3 to 5 minutes.

6. Add cauliflower or brussels sprouts and peas or cooked lima beans. Stir and cook over medium-low heat for 2 minutes, until vegetables are tender. Be careful not to overcook the cauliflower.

## VARIATION:

Another good combination is potatoes, cauliflower, Brussels sprouts, and lima beans. Cut all vegetables in same small size to cook evenly. Adjust the ground spices according to your taste.

## NUTRITION PER SERVING

| | | |
|---|---|---|
| 98 calories | 0 mg cholesterol | 2 g fiber |
| 5 g fat | 110 mg sodium | 2 g protein |
| 0.4 g saturated fat | 11 g carbohydrate | 293 mg potassium |

# ROASTED POTATO MEDLEY

*Give your roasted potatoes an extra zing with this recipe! Yukon Gold and sweet potatoes seasoned with turmeric, cayenne, and garlic are bursting with flavor in this side dish. It makes an excellent accompaniment to any meat or vegetable dish.*

## INGREDIENTS

¾ pound Yukon Gold potatoes, peeled and cut into cubes (1½ cups)

¾ pound sweet potatoes, peeled and cut into cubes (1½ cups)

¼ cup water

½ teaspoon ground turmeric

⅛ teaspoon salt (more or less to taste)

¼ teaspoon cayenne pepper (more or less to taste)

2 tablespoons oil

2 garlic cloves, chopped

¼ cup chopped green onions

Yield: 3 cups
Serving size: ½ cup

1. Place all cubed potatoes in a glass bowl with ¼ cup water. Partially cook for 2 minutes in microwave. (Or boil/steam for 5 minutes on stovetop.) Potatoes should still be firm.

2. Mix together turmeric, salt, and cayenne pepper. Sprinkle on potatoes and toss until evenly coated with spices.

3. Heat oil in a skillet over medium-high heat (the oil should be hot but not smoking). Add the seasoned potato pieces and garlic to skillet. Cook over medium-low heat for 3 to 5 minutes, stirring to prevent sticking, until potatoes become golden and crisp. (Alternatively, you can spread the potatoes and garlic on a dark baking sheet and bake at 425°F until crisp.)

4. Add green onions, stir, and serve.

## NUTRITION PER SERVING

| | | |
|---|---|---|
| 110 calories | 0 mg cholesterol | 2 g fiber |
| 4.5 g fat | 70 mg sodium | 2 g protein |
| 0 g saturated fat | 15 g carbohydrate | 122 mg potassium |

# SEASONED MASHED POTATOES

*If you're tired of basic mashed potatoes, try this version enhanced with the subtle flavors of ginger, chili, and spices. This versatile side dish makes a great sandwich filler when spread with chutney on toasted gluten-free bread. It's also a delicious topping on gluten-free crackers, and of course, a creative side dish for Thanksgiving.*

## INGREDIENTS

2 medium Russet potatoes, peeled and cubed (2 cups)

½ teaspoon ground turmeric (divided)

1 tablespoon oil

½ teaspoon black mustard seeds

½ teaspoon cumin seeds

½ cup chopped onion

¼ cup chopped tomato

1 fresh green chili pepper, chopped (more or less to taste)

½ tablespoon grated fresh ginger

⅛ teaspoon cayenne pepper (more or less to taste)

¼ teaspoon salt (more or less to taste)

¼ cup minced fresh cilantro

Yield: 2 cups

Serving size: ½ cup

1. Place potatoes in a 2-quart saucepan. Add enough water to cover potatoes. Add ¼ teaspoon turmeric and bring to a boil. Reduce to a simmer and cook about 20 minutes or until potatoes are tender when pierced with a fork. Drain and discard water. Reserve potatoes.

2. Heat oil in a skillet over medium-high heat (the oil should be hot but not smoking). Add mustard seeds and cumin seeds and stir until mustard seeds start to pop and cumin seeds change color from light brown to semi-dark brown.

3. Add onion, tomato, and green chili pepper. Cook for 1 minute while stirring. Add remaining ¼ teaspoon turmeric, ginger, cayenne pepper, and salt. Stir to blend.

4. Add potatoes and mash as they cook over medium heat for 2 to 3 minutes.

5. Add cilantro, mix, and serve.

## NUTRITION PER SERVING

| | | |
|---|---|---|
| 120 calories | 0 mg cholesterol | 2 g fiber |
| 3.5 g fat | 150 mg sodium | 2 g protein |
| 0.5 g saturated fat | 20 g carbohydrate | 415 mg potassium |

# POTATOES IN ONION AND TOMATO SAUCE

*This hearty tomato-based sauce with potatoes makes an excellent side dish.*

## INGREDIENTS

1 tablespoon oil

1 bay leaf

1 teaspoon black mustard seeds

½ teaspoon cumin seeds

½ medium onion, sliced lengthwise (about ½ cup)

½ cup chopped tomato

½ pound potatoes, scrubbed and cut in ½ inch x 1 inch oblong pieces (1½ cups)

¼ teaspoon ground turmeric

½ cup no-salt-added tomato sauce

1 teaspoon ground cumin

⅛ teaspoon ground cinnamon

½ teaspoon cayenne pepper (more or less to taste)

¼ teaspoon salt (more or less to taste)

1½ cups hot water

¼ cup chopped fresh cilantro

Yield: 3 cups
Serving size: ½ cup

1. Heat oil in a skillet over medium heat (the oil should be hot but not smoking). Add bay leaf, mustard seeds, and cumin seeds and stir until mustard seeds start to pop and cumin seeds change color from light brown to semi-dark brown.

2. Add onion, tomato, potatoes, and turmeric to saucepan. Stir and cook over medium-low heat for 1 to 2 minutes.

3. Stir in tomato sauce, ground cumin, cinnamon, cayenne pepper, and salt. Bring to a simmer. Add 1½ cups hot water and cilantro; stir to combine. Cover and cook over medium-low heat about 8 to 10 minutes, stirring occasionally, until potatoes are tender.

## VARIATION:

Omit potatoes and increase both onions and tomatoes to 1 cup each to create a delicious Onion and Tomato Sauce.

## NUTRITION PER SERVING

| | | |
|---|---|---|
| 80 calorie | 0 mg cholesterol | 1 g fiber |
| 2.5 g fat | 113 mg sodium | 1 g protein |
| 0 g saturated fat | 13 g carbohydrate | 276 mg potassium |

# SEASONED POTATOES IN LENTIL SAUCE

*The delicate flavors of the spices and tomatoes bring this potato-and-lentil dish to life. It makes a great accompaniment to roasted chicken or grilled shrimp, and can also be served over plain rice or quinoa.*

## INGREDIENTS

3 cups water

½ cup split mung beans (moong dal)

¾ teaspoon ground turmeric (divided)

3 tablespoons oil

1 whole dried red chili pepper (more or less to taste)

1 teaspoon cumin seeds

½ cup chopped onion

1 cup chopped tomato

1 teaspoon ground cumin

½ teaspoon cayenne pepper (more or less to taste)

1 cup scrubbed and cubed potatoes

¼ teaspoon salt (more or less to taste)

½ cup chopped fresh cilantro

½ cup warm water (optional)

Yield: 4 cups
Serving size: 1 cup

1. Bring 3 cups water to a boil in a 1-quart saucepan. Add mung beans and ¼ teaspoon turmeric. Reduce heat to medium and cook, uncovered, for about 30 minutes, until beans soften. If water evaporates during the cooking process, add another ½ cup. Do not drain. Mash mung beans with a potato masher. Reserve.

2. Heat oil in a skillet over medium-high heat (the oil should be hot but not smoking). Add red chili pepper and cumin seeds. Stir until cumin seeds change color from light brown to semi-dark brown.

3. Add onion, tomato, ground cumin, cayenne pepper, and remaining ½ teaspoon turmeric. Cook about 2 to 3 minutes or until onion is tender.

4. Add reserved mashed mung beans, cubed potatoes, salt, and cilantro; stir to combine. Bring to a simmer. Reduce heat to low and simmer about 3 to 5 minutes, stirring occasionally and adding ½ cup of warm water, if needed, until potatoes are tender.

## NUTRITION PER SERVING

| | | |
|---|---|---|
| 170 calories | 0 mg cholesterol | 1 g fiber |
| 11 g fat | 150 mg sodium | 4 g protein |
| 1 g saturated fat | 14 g carbohydrate | 117 mg potassium |

# SWEET POTATOES WITH COCONUT

*A simple, savory way to prepare sweet potatoes with delicate seasonings, this is a delicious side dish with poultry.*

## INGREDIENTS

1 pound sweet potatoes, peeled and cubed (about 2 cups)

1 tablespoon oil

1 whole dried red chili pepper

1 teaspoon black mustard seeds

½ teaspoon cumin seeds

½ green chili pepper, chopped (more or less to taste)

¼ teaspoon salt (more or less to taste)

2 tablespoons grated fresh coconut or unsweetened shredded dried coconut

Yield: 1⅔ cups

Serving size: ⅓ cup

1. Steam cubed sweet potatoes about 5 minutes or until tender. Set aside.

2. Heat oil in a skillet over medium heat (the oil should be hot but not smoking). Add red chili pepper, mustard seeds, and cumin seeds. Stir until mustard seeds start to pop and cumin seeds change color to light brown.

3. Add steamed sweet potatoes, green chili pepper, and salt. Gently mix with the seasonings for 1 to 2 minutes.

4. Add coconut and gently mix. Serve warm.

## NUTRITION PER SERVING

| | | |
|---|---|---|
| 100 calories | 0 mg cholesterol | 3 g fiber |
| 1.5 g fat | 170 mg sodium | 2 g protein |
| 1 g saturated fat | 19 g carbohydrate | 335 mg potassium |

# SPINACH IN LENTIL SAUCE

*This mild and subtly-flavored spinach-and-lentil dish can be served as a sauce over quinoa or rice or as a side dish.*

## INGREDIENTS

4 cups water

1 cup split mung beans (moong dal)

¼ teaspoon ground turmeric

¼ cup chopped onion

1 tablespoon minced garlic

3 tablespoons grated fresh ginger

1 (10-ounce) package frozen chopped spinach, thawed

2 tablespoons ground cumin

¼ teaspoon salt (more or less to taste)

¼ teaspoon cayenne pepper, or
½ fresh green chili pepper, minced (more or less to taste)

1 garlic clove, crushed

Yield: 5 cups

Serving size: ½ cup

1. Bring 4 cups water to a boil in a 1-quart saucepan. Add mung beans and turmeric. Reduce heat to medium and cook, uncovered, for about 20 minutes or until beans soften and become creamy. If water evaporates during the cooking process, add another cup. Do not drain.

2. Stir in onion, minced garlic, and ginger. Cover and cook over medium heat, stirring occasionally, about 2 minutes.

3. Stir in spinach, cumin, salt, cayenne pepper or green chili pepper, and crushed garlic. Bring to a simmer, cover, and cook about 1 to 2 minutes over medium-low heat, stirring occasionally, until spinach is tender.

## NUTRITION PER SERVING

| | | |
|---|---|---|
| 90 calories | 0 mg cholesterol | 2 g fiber |
| 0.5 g fat | 85 mg sodium | 6 g protein |
| 0 g saturated fat | 14 g carbohydrate | 121 mg potassium |

# SPINACH WITH LENTILS AND COCONUT

*This colorful, wholesome spinach blend can be served as a side dish or used to make Spinach Lentil Rice (page 99) or Stuffed Baby Portabella Mushrooms (page 39).*

## INGREDIENTS

2 cups water

¼ teaspoon ground turmeric

½ cup split mung beans (moong dal)

1 tablespoon oil

1 teaspoon cumin seeds

1 cup chopped onion

2 tablespoons chopped garlic

1 fresh green chili pepper, chopped (more or less to taste)

1 (10-ounce) package frozen chopped spinach, thawed, or 1½ pounds fresh baby spinach, chopped

¼ teaspoon ground cumin

¾ teaspoon garam masala

¼ teaspoon salt (more or less to taste)

2 tablespoons grated fresh coconut or unsweetened shredded dried coconut

Yield: 4 cups

Serving size: ½ cup

1. Bring 2 cups water to a boil. Add the turmeric and mung beans and cook partially uncovered until soft, about 15 minutes. If water evaporates before mung beans become tender, add an additional ¼ cup. Do not drain; reserve.

2. Heat oil in a skillet over medium heat (the oil should be hot but not smoking). Add cumin seeds and stir until seeds change color from light brown to semi-dark brown.

3. Add onion, garlic, and chili pepper; cook for 1 minute while stirring.

4. Add spinach, ground cumin, garam masala, and salt. Stir well, cover, and cook over medium heat about 3 minutes or until spinach is tender, stirring occasionally.

5. Add reserved cooked mung beans mixture to spinach mixture. Stir thoroughly and heat to serving temperature.

6. Add coconut, stir, and serve.

## NUTRITION PER SERVING

| | | |
|---|---|---|
| 100 calories | 0 mg cholesterol | 2 g fiber |
| 3 g fat | 135 mg sodium | 5 g protein |
| 1 g saturated fat | 12 g carbohydrate | 176 mg potassium |

# BUTTERNUT SQUASH WITH CILANTRO

*In this flavorful side dish, Indian spices pair wonderfully with butternut squash, a vegetable packed with vitamins A and C.*

Yield: 2 cups

Serving size: ½ cup

## INGREDIENTS

1 pound butternut squash*

2 teaspoons oil

1 teaspoon black mustard seeds

½ teaspoon cumin seeds

½ medium onion, sliced lengthwise (about ½ cup)

½ cup chopped tomato

½ teaspoon ground turmeric

¼ teaspoon cayenne pepper (more or less to taste)

½ teaspoon ground cumin

¼ teaspoon salt (more or less to taste)

¼ cup no-salt-added tomato sauce

2 tablespoons grated fresh coconut or unsweetened shredded dried coconut

2 tablespoons chopped fresh cilantro

---

*Peeled, pre-cut squash is available in some grocery stores. You need about 2 cups.

1. Cut the squash in half lengthwise and remove seeds. Cut in slices crosswise, peel, and cut into 1-inch cubes (about 2 cups). Reserve.

2. Heat oil in a skillet over medium-high heat (the oil should be hot but not smoking). Add mustard seeds and cumin seeds and stir until mustard seeds start to pop.

3. Add onion and tomato and cook for 1 minute while stirring.

4. Add turmeric, cayenne pepper, ground cumin, salt, and tomato sauce; stir and bring to a boil.

5. Add reserved squash, cover, and cook over medium heat for 5 to 7 minutes or until tender when pierced with a fork (add water a tablespoon at a time if needed).

6. Add coconut and cilantro, gently stir and serve warm.

## NUTRITION PER SERVING

| | | |
|---|---|---|
| 170 calories | 0 mg cholesterol | 4 g fiber |
| 11 g fat | 160 mg sodium | 2 g protein |
| 3 g saturated fat | 19 g carbohydrate | 598 mg potassium |

# BUTTERNUT SQUASH AND CHICKPEA CURRY

*Squash and chickpeas come together in a flavorful sauce in this complete and satisfying vegetarian meal. Serve over rice.*

Yield: 4 cups
Serving size: 1 cup

## INGREDIENTS

1 tablespoon oil

1 bay leaf

¼ teaspoon fennel seeds

½ teaspoon cumin seeds

½ cup chopped onion

¼ cup chopped tomato

6 cloves garlic, quartered

2 tablespoons grated fresh ginger

3 cups peeled and cubed butternut squash*

1 (15-ounce) can chickpeas, drained and rinsed (about 1½ cups)

1 to 2 cups no-salt-added tomato sauce

½ teaspoon ground turmeric

¼ teaspoon ground cinnamon

2 teaspoons curry powder

1 teaspoon garam masala

½ teaspoon Black Pepper Cumin Powder (page 9)

⅛ teaspoon salt (more or less to taste)

¼ cup chopped fresh cilantro

¼ cup canned coconut milk (optional)

*Peeled, pre-cut squash is available in some grocery stores.

1. Heat oil in deep skillet over medium-high heat (the oil should be hot but not smoking). Add bay leaf, fennel seeds, and cumin seeds and stir until cumin seeds change color from light brown to semi-dark brown.

2. Add onion, tomato, garlic, and ginger and cook 1 to 2 minutes while stirring.

3. Add squash, chickpeas, 1 cup tomato sauce, turmeric, cinnamon, curry powder, garam masala, Black Pepper Cumin Powder, and salt. Bring to a simmer, cover, and cook over medium-low heat, stirring occasionally, about 15 to 20 minutes or until squash is tender. Thin sauce with additional tomato sauce or water if desired.

4. Stir in cilantro and coconut milk, if using. Cook 2 minutes and serve.

## VARIATION:

Substitute low-sodium Spicy V-8 juice for half of the tomato sauce.

## NUTRITION PER SERVING WITHOUT COCONUT MILK

| | | |
|---|---|---|
| 260 calories | 0 mg cholesterol | 10 g fiber |
| 6 g fat | 95 mg sodium | 9 g protein |
| 0.5 g saturated fat | 48 g carbohydrate | 1,158 mg potassium |

## NUTRITION PER SERVING WITH COCONUT MILK

| | | |
|---|---|---|
| 290 calories | 0 mg cholesterol | 11 g fiber |
| 9 g fat | 100 mg sodium | 9 g protein |
| 3 g saturated fat | 48 g carbohydrate | 1,189 mg potassium |

# SPICED SPAGHETTI SQUASH

*In this delightful vegetable dish, strands of spaghetti squash are tossed with sautéed mustard seeds and cumin seeds and fragrant, flavor-enhancing garam masala.*

## INGREDIENTS

1 (3-pound) spaghetti squash

1 tablespoon oil

1 teaspoon black mustard seeds

1 teaspoon cumin seeds

½ cup chopped onion

½ fresh green chili pepper, minced (more or less to taste)

½ teaspoon garam masala

¼ teaspoon salt (more or less to taste)

¼ cup chopped fresh cilantro

2 small whole red chilies (optional for garnish)

Yield: 4 cups

Serving size: ½ cup

1. Cut squash in half lengthwise and remove seeds. Place on a plate, cut side down, and microwave on high 10 to 12 minutes or until soft. Let cool slightly. Using a fork, pull the flesh lengthwise to separate it into long strands. Reserve 4 cups of squash. (Save any remaining squash for another time or freeze.)

2. Heat oil in a skillet over medium-high heat (the oil should be hot but not smoking). Add mustard seeds and cumin seeds and stir until mustard seeds start to pop and cumin seeds change color from light brown to semi-dark brown.

3. Add onion, chili pepper, garam masala, and salt. Sauté for 2 to 3 minutes, until onions are tender.

4. Add the 4 cups of squash and toss to coat with the seasonings.

5. Place in serving dish and garnish with cilantro and red chilies, if using.

## NUTRITION PER SERVING

| | | |
|---|---|---|
| 45 calories | 0 mg cholesterol | 1 g fiber |
| 2 g fat | 90 mg sodium | 1 g protein |
| 0 g saturated fat | 7 g carbohydrate | 134 mg potassium |

# SUMMER SQUASH MEDLEY

*Zucchini and yellow squash are abundant in gardens and farmers markets in the summertime. Here is a way to use up the garden's bounty in a tasty and colorful side dish.*

## INGREDIENTS

1 tablespoon oil

1 whole dried red chili pepper

½ teaspoon black mustard seeds

½ teaspoon cumin seeds

1½ cups cubed zucchini

1½ cups cubed yellow squash

¼ teaspoon ground turmeric

½ fresh green chili pepper, minced (more or less to taste)

¼ teaspoon salt (more or less to taste)

2 tablespoons grated fresh coconut or unsweetened shredded dried coconut

Yield: 2½ cups

Serving size: ½ cup

1. Heat oil in a skillet over medium-high heat (the oil should be hot but not smoking). Add red chili pepper, mustard seeds, and cumin seeds and stir until mustard seeds start to pop and cumin seeds change color from light brown to semi-dark brown.

2. Add zucchini, yellow squash, turmeric, green chili pepper, and salt. Cook over medium-low heat for 2 minutes while stirring.

3. Add coconut, stir, and serve.

## NUTRITION PER SERVING

| | | |
|---|---|---|
| 50 calories | 0 mg cholesterol | 1 g fiber |
| 4.5 g fat | 125 mg sodium | 1 g protein |
| 1.5 g saturated fat | 4 g carbohydrate | 229 mg potassium |

# SWISS CHARD LENTIL CRUMBLE

*Colorful Swiss chard is combined with split peas and coconut in this hearty vegetable dish.*

### INGREDIENTS

⅓ cup yellow or green split peas

1¼ cups hot water (divided)

1 whole dried red chili pepper (more or less to taste)

½ teaspoon fennel seeds

2 teaspoons cumin seeds (divided)

3 tablespoons oil

1 teaspoon black mustard seeds

1 cup chopped onion

½ teaspoon ground turmeric

½ teaspoon cayenne pepper (more or less to taste)

¼ teaspoon salt (more or less to taste)

4 cups chopped Swiss chard (including stems)

3 tablespoons grated fresh coconut or unsweetened shredded dried coconut

Yield: 4 cups

Serving size: ½ cup

1. Place split peas in a bowl with 1 cup hot water. Let soak for 30 minutes. Drain.

2. Place drained peas in a blender or food processor with remaining ¼ cup hot water, red chili pepper, fennel seeds, and 1 teaspoon cumin seeds. Blend or process until the texture of coarse cornmeal.

3. Pour mixture in a microwave-safe dish, cover with paper towel, and microwave on high for 3 minutes. Mixture will feel somewhat firm. Cool for 5 minutes; break into small pieces with fork; reserve.

4. Heat oil in a skillet over medium-high heat (the oil should be hot but not smoking). Add mustard seeds and remaining 1 teaspoon cumin seeds and stir until mustard seeds start to pop and cumin seeds change color from light brown to semi-dark brown.

5. Add onion and cook for 30 seconds while stirring.

6. Add reserved split pea mixture, turmeric, cayenne pepper, and salt. Stir well. Continue to cook over medium-low heat for 3 to 5 minutes while stirring, until the split peas become golden and grainy in texture.

7. Stir in Swiss chard, cover, and cook over low heat until chard becomes tender, stirring frequently.

8. Add coconut, stir, and serve.

## VARIATIONS:

Instead of Swiss chard use:
- baby spinach to make Spinach Lentil Crumble
- chopped broccoli to make Broccoli Lentil Crumble
- shredded carrots to make Carrot Lentil Crumble
- diced green beans to make Green Bean Lentil Crumble
- chopped kale to make Kale Lentil Crumble

## NUTRITION PER SERVING

| | | |
|---|---|---|
| 100 calories | 0 mg cholesterol | 3 g fiber |
| 7 g fat | 115 mg sodium | 3 g protein |
| 1.5 g saturated fat | 8 g carbohydrate | 121 mg potassium |

# ROASTED VEGETABLES

*Nothing beats the simple appeal of a colorful blend of roasted vegetables in a light seasoning.*

## INGREDIENTS

4 tablespoons oil

1 teaspoon ground cumin

½ teaspoon ground coriander

¼ teaspoon cayenne pepper (more or less to taste)

¼ teaspoon salt (more or less to taste)

5 cups raw vegetables, cut into pieces, such as:

  1 cup broccoli florets, cut in half

  1 cup cauliflower florets, cut in half

  1 cup brussels sprouts, stem ends sliced off and cut in half

  1 small sweet potato, peeled and cut in cubes (about 1 cup)

  1 cup peeled and cubed butternut squash

Yield: 3½ cups

Serving size: ½ cup

1. Preheat oven to 425°F.

2. In large bowl, combine oil, cumin, coriander, cayenne pepper, and salt.

3. Add vegetables and toss to coat. Spread out in a single layer on a dark baking sheet. (If they are too close to each other, they will steam instead of roasting. Dark baking sheets work best to brown vegetables.)

4. Place in oven and roast 10 minutes. Check to see if they are starting to brown. If not, return to oven for 5 more minutes. When edges are browned, stir and bake 10 minutes longer or until vegetables reach desired softness. Cooking time will vary based on your individual oven and how well done you like your vegetables.

## NUTRITION PER SERVING

| | | |
|---|---|---|
| 120 calories | 0 mg cholesterol | 3 g fiber |
| 8 g fat | 110 mg sodium | 2 g protein |
| 0.5 g saturated fat | 10 g carbohydrate | 266 mg potassium |

# FISH & SHRIMP DISHES

# FISH IN GINGER-GARLIC SAUCE

*Most types of fish lend themselves beautifully to Indian spices. Here the flavors of garlic, chili, ginger, and a range of spices make the fish irresistible. Use any firm fish such as halibut, red snapper, striped bass, catfish, haddock, pollock, salmon, tilapia, or whitefish.*

## INGREDIENTS

2 tablespoons oil

½ teaspoon fennel seeds

½ teaspoon cumin seeds

½ cup chopped onion

¼ cup chopped tomato

6 garlic cloves, quartered

½ fresh green chili pepper, chopped (more or less to taste)

½ teaspoon ground turmeric

¼ teaspoon cayenne pepper (more or less to taste)

1 teaspoon ground cumin

½ teaspoon garam masala

½ teaspoon Black Pepper Cumin Powder (page 9)

¼ teaspoon salt (more or less to taste)

1 cup no-salt-added tomato sauce

½ cup warm water

2 tablespoons grated fresh ginger

½ pound boneless skinless fish fillets, cut into pieces

1 tablespoon chopped fresh cilantro

Yield: 3 cups

Serving size: ¾ cup

1. Heat oil in a skillet over medium-high heat (the oil should be hot but not smoking). Add fennel seeds and cumin seeds and stir until seeds change color from light brown to semi-dark brown.

2. Add onion, tomato, garlic, chili pepper, and turmeric. Cook for 1 to 2 minutes while stirring.

3. Add cayenne pepper, ground cumin, garam masala, Black Pepper Cumin Powder, and salt.

4. Add tomato sauce and warm water. Bring to a boil and then reduce to a simmer. Add ginger. Cook, uncovered, for 5 minutes.

5. Add fish pieces and cook over medium-low heat, spooning sauce over fish occasionally, until fish is opaque in the center, about 5 to 7 minutes.

6. Serve garnished with cilantro.

## NUTRITION PER SERVING

| | | |
|---|---|---|
| 310 calories | 55 mg cholesterol | 4 g fiber |
| 17 g fat | 376 mg sodium | 26 g protein |
| 2 g saturated fat | 17 g carbohydrate | 976 mg potassium |

# SALMON AND QUINOA PATTIES

*Made with quinoa and enticing spices, these salmon patties are packed with flavor and nutrition. An easy-to-prepare and creative way to boost your intake of omega-3s. Serve with Cilantro Chutney (page 45).*

## INGREDIENTS

¼ cup dry quinoa

½ cup hot water

8 ounces wild salmon, skin removed

2 handfuls fresh cilantro

1 teaspoon grated fresh ginger

¼ teaspoon Black Pepper Cumin Powder (page 9)

½ teaspoon garam masala

⅛ teaspoon salt (more or less to taste)

Yield: 4 patties

Serving size: 1 patty

1. Prepare quinoa with the ½ cup hot water as directed on page 11 (you should have ½ cup cooked quinoa).

2. Cut salmon into ¼-inch square pieces; reserve.

3. Place cilantro in food processor and pulse until chopped. Add cooked quinoa, cubed salmon, ginger, Black Pepper Cumin Powder, garam masala, and salt. Pulse several times until coarsely chopped. (Do not over process; it should not be smooth.) Form mixture into 4 patties. Brush with oil.

4. Heat skillet or grill pan over medium-high heat. Add patties and cook about 2 to 3 minutes per side or until golden brown.

5. Serve patties with chutney if desired.

## NUTRITION PER SERVING

| | | |
|---|---|---|
| 110 calories | 25 mg cholesterol | 1 g fiber |
| 4 g fat | 130 mg sodium | 13 g protein |
| 1 g saturated fat | 5 g carbohydrate | 317 mg potassium |

# SPICE-RUBBED SEARED FISH

*The robust flavors in this spice blend are delicious when rubbed on your favorite firm-fleshed fish, but work nicely with meats too.*

## INGREDIENTS

½ pound boneless skinless fish fillets (use any firm fish such as halibut, red snapper, striped bass, catfish, haddock, salmon, or whitefish)

2 tablespoons oil

1 tablespoon chopped fresh cilantro

### SPICE RUB

¾ teaspoon ground turmeric

¼ teaspoon cayenne pepper (more or less to taste)

1 teaspoon ground cumin

¼ teaspoon ground coriander

¼ teaspoon salt (more or less to taste)

1 tablespoon finely minced garlic

1 tablespoon finely minced ginger

1 teaspoon fresh lemon juice

Yield: 8 ounces
Serving size: 4 ounces

1. Wipe fish with paper towels.

2. Mix spice rub ingredients together in a bowl. Rub the spice mixture all over the fish fillets. Cover and marinate in the refrigerator for 20 minutes.

3. Heat oil in a skillet over medium-high heat (the oil should be hot but not smoking). Add fish to the skillet in a single layer, making sure pieces do not touch or they will steam and not brown. Pan-sear the fish until golden brown, about 3 to 5 minutes per side. Place on paper towels to absorb any excess oil. (Alternatively, spray fish with oil and broil on high.)

4. Meanwhile, heat a plate for serving the fish. If your plate is microwave-safe, microwaving it on high for a minute will work. Serve fish on warm plate garnished with cilantro.

## NUTRITION PER SERVING

| | | |
|---|---|---|
| 200 calories | 35 mg cholesterol | 1 g fiber |
| 10 g fat | 260 mg sodium | 24 g protein |
| 1 g saturated fat | 1 g carbohydrate | 538 mg potassium |

# ZESTY SALMON SLICES

*The subtle combination of spices in this spice paste enhances the flavor of salmon without too much heat.*

## INGREDIENTS

8 ounces wild salmon fillet

### SPICE PASTE

½ teaspoon ground turmeric

½ teaspoon Black Pepper Cumin Powder (page 9)

¼ teaspoon salt (more or less to taste)

1 teaspoon fennel seeds, ground in mortar or coffee grinder

1 teaspoon fresh lemon juice

1 tablespoon oil

Yield: 8 ounces

Serving size: 4 ounces

1. Remove skin from salmon. Slice salmon thinly. (If the salmon is slightly frozen, it is easier to cut in slices.)

2. Combine spice paste ingredients in a small bowl.

3. Pat salmon slices with spice paste. Cover and refrigerate for 20 to 30 minutes.

4. Heat a non-stick skillet on medium-high heat. Pan-sear salmon until golden brown, about 2 to 3 minutes per side.

5. Meanwhile, heat a plate for serving the fish. If your plate is microwave-safe, microwaving it on high for a minute will work. Serve salmon on warm plate.

## NUTRITION PER SERVING

| | | |
|---|---|---|
| 260 calories | 70 mg cholesterol | 1 g fiber |
| 17 g fat | 350 mg sodium | 24 g protein |
| 2.5 g saturated fat | 1 g carbohydrate | 472 mg potassium |

# SPICY SEARED SHRIMP

*This seared shrimp dish is bursting with the subtle flavors of fennel, ginger, and other seasonings. A quick, easy-to-prepare meal that can be served with rice and salad.*

## INGREDIENTS

½ pound fresh large raw shrimp

2 tablespoons oil

¼ teaspoon cumin seeds

¼ teaspoon fennel seeds

¼ cup chopped onion

1 tablespoon minced garlic

1 tablespoon grated fresh ginger

¼ teaspoon ground turmeric

3 tablespoons no-salt-added tomato sauce

½ tablespoon gluten-free chili-garlic sauce

¼ teaspoon salt (more or less to taste)

2 tablespoons cilantro, minced

Yield: 14 shrimp

Serving size: 7 shrimp

1. Peel and devein the shrimp. To devein, make a shallow cut lengthwise down the outer curve of the shrimp's body and remove the dark ribbon-like string. Rinse, pat dry with paper towel, and reserve.

2. Heat oil in a skillet over medium-high heat (the oil should be hot but not smoking). Add cumin seeds and fennel seeds and stir until seeds change color from light brown to semi-dark brown.

3. Add onion, garlic, ginger, and turmeric. Cook 2 to 3 minutes, while stirring, until onion is translucent. Stir in tomato sauce, chili-garlic paste, and salt.

4. Add shrimp and sauté about 2 to 3 minutes, until flesh changes from gray translucent to pink. Do not overcook as shrimp toughen quickly.

5. Garnish with cilantro and serve warm.

## NUTRITION PER SERVING

| | | |
|---|---|---|
| 350 calories | 350 mg cholesterol | 0 g fiber |
| 17 g fat | 825 mg sodium | 35 g protein |
| 0 g saturated fat | 5 g carbohydrate | 448 mg potassium |

# POULTRY, EGG & LAMB DISHES

# CHICKEN IN COCONUT ALMOND SAUCE

*A rich, fragrant coconut almond sauce envelopes tender chunks of chicken. This is a chicken curry like no other! Serve over rice or quinoa.*

Yield: 4 cups
Serving size: 1 cup

## INGREDIENTS

1 pound skinless boneless chicken breasts or thighs

1½ tablespoons oil

1 bay leaf

½ teaspoon cumin seeds

½ teaspoon fennel seeds

½ medium onion, sliced lengthwise

½ cup chopped tomato

½ teaspoon ground turmeric

½ teaspoon curry powder

¼ teaspoon ground cinnamon

½ teaspoon ground cardamom (optional)

½ teaspoon salt (more or less to taste)

¼ cup minced fresh cilantro

### SPICE PASTE

2 small slices fresh ginger

1 fresh green chili pepper

1 clove garlic

1 teaspoon fennel seeds

1 tablespoon poppy seeds

2 teaspoons cumin seeds

10 raw almonds (½-ounce)

⅓ cup grated fresh coconut or unsweetened shredded dried coconut

1 cup hot water

1. Wipe chicken with a damp paper towel. Cut into 2-inch pieces. Reserve.

2. Place spice paste ingredients in a food processor or blender. Process for about 5 minutes into a smooth paste. Reserve.

3. Heat oil in a skillet over medium-high heat (the oil should be hot but not smoking). Add bay leaf, cumin seeds, and fennel seeds and stir until seeds change color from light brown to semi-dark brown.

4. Add onion, tomato, and turmeric and cook for about 2 to 3 minutes while stirring.

5. Add reserved chicken and sauté over medium-high heat for 3 to 5 minutes, until chicken starts to brown.

6. Stir in curry powder, cinnamon, cardamom (if using), salt, and reserved spice paste. Bring to a simmer. Cover and cook over medium-low heat, stirring occasionally, about 15 to 20 minutes or until chicken is tender.

7. Add cilantro and cook for 1 minute.

## NUTRITION PER SERVING USING CHICKEN THIGHS

| | | |
|---|---|---|
| 260 calories | 85 mg cholesterol | 3 g fiber |
| 15 g fat | 360 mg sodium | 23 g protein |
| 5 g saturated fat | 8 g carbohydrate | 381 mg potassium |

## NUTRITION PER SERVING USING CHICKEN BREASTS

| | | |
|---|---|---|
| 250 calories | 60 mg cholesterol | 3 g fiber |
| 12 g fat | 340 mg sodium | 26 g protein |
| 4 g saturated fat | 8 g carbohydrate | 488 mg potassium |

# CHICKEN WITH POTATOES IN GINGER-GARLIC SAUCE

*A classic chicken curry in an aromatic ginger-garlic sauce can't be beat. Serve over rice or quinoa for a complete meal.*

Yield: 4 cups

Serving size: 1 cup

## INGREDIENTS

1 pound boneless or with bone skinless chicken breasts or thighs

2 tablespoons oil

1 bay leaf

½ teaspoon cumin seeds

¼ teaspoon fennel seeds

2 (½-inch each) slivers cinnamon stick

½ cup chopped onion

½ cup chopped tomato

6 cloves garlic, quartered

2 tablespoons grated fresh ginger

½ teaspoon ground turmeric

2 teaspoons curry powder

½ teaspoon Black Pepper Cumin Powder (page 9)

1 teaspoon garam masala

¼ teaspoon salt (more or less to taste)

1 cup cubed potatoes (Yukon Gold or fingerling)

1 cup no-salt-added tomato sauce

¼ cup chopped fresh cilantro

1. Wipe chicken with a damp paper towel. Cut into pieces; reserve.

2. Heat oil in a skillet over medium-high heat (the oil should be hot but not smoking). Add bay leaf, cumin seeds, fennel seeds, and cinnamon slivers. Stir until cumin seeds change color from light brown to semi-dark brown.

3. Add onion, tomato, garlic, ginger, and turmeric. Cook for 2 to 3 minutes while stirring. Add chicken and cook over medium-high heat for 3 to 5 minutes.

4. Stir in curry powder, Black Pepper Cumin Powder, garam masala, and salt. Add potatoes and tomato sauce. Bring to a simmer. Cover and cook over medium-low heat about 15 to 20 minutes, stirring occasionally and adding ½ to 1 cup water, if needed, until potatoes and chicken are tender.

5. Add cilantro and cook 1 minute.

## VARIATION:

Use lamb instead of chicken to prepare **Lamb with Potatoes in Ginger Garlic Sauce**.

| NUTRITION PER SERVING USING CHICKEN THIGHS | | |
|---|---|---|
| 240 calories | 95 mg cholesterol | 2 g fiber |
| 12 g fat | 360 mg sodium | 23 g protein |
| 1.5 g saturated fat | 9 g carbohydrate | 381 mg potassium |

| NUTRITION PER SERVING USING CHICKEN BREASTS | | |
|---|---|---|
| 230 calories | 65 mg cholesterol | 2 g fiber |
| 9 g fat | 280 mg sodium | 28 g protein |
| 1 g saturated fat | 10 g carbohydrate | 634 mg potassium |

# PEPPER CHICKEN

*Tender pieces of chicken seasoned with garlic, ginger, and pepper. You can serve this recipe on its own or use to make Chicken Rice Pilaf (page 207).*

## INGREDIENTS

1 pound boneless skinless chicken thighs or breasts

2 tablespoons oil

1 whole dried red chili pepper (more or less to taste)

1 bay leaf

3 (½-inch each) slivers cinnamon stick

½ teaspoon cumin seeds

½ teaspoon fennel seeds

½ cup chopped onion

1 tablespoon grated fresh ginger

4 garlic cloves, quartered

½ teaspoon ground turmeric

1½ teaspoons Black Pepper Cumin Powder (page 9)

1 teaspoon garam masala

1 teaspoon curry powder

¼ teaspoon salt (more or less to taste)

¼ small red onion, cut lengthwise into 1-inch pieces

2 tablespoons fresh cilantro

Yield: 2 cups

Serving size: ½ cup

1. Cut chicken into bite-size pieces and reserve.

2. Heat oil in a skillet over medium-high heat (the oil should be hot but not smoking). Add red chili pepper, bay leaf, cinnamon slivers, cumin seeds, and fennel seeds. Stir until cumin seeds change color from light brown to semi-dark brown.

3. Add onion, ginger, garlic, and turmeric. Cook for 2 to 3 minutes while stirring.

4. Add reserved chicken to skillet and cook over medium-high heat for 2 to 3 minutes until chicken begins to turn opaque.

5. Add Black Pepper Cumin Powder, garam masala, curry powder, and salt. Cover and cook over medium-low heat, stirring occasionally, and adding about 1 tablespoon of water, if needed, until chicken is tender, about 15 to 20 minutes.

6. Garnish with red onion and cilantro.

## NUTRITION PER SERVING USING CHICKEN THIGHS

| | | |
|---|---|---|
| 260 calories | 70 mg cholesterol | 1 g fiber |
| 17 g fat | 357 mg sodium | 23 g protein |
| 3 g saturated fat | 6 g carbohydrate | 148 mg potassium |

## NUTRITION PER SERVING USING CHICKEN BREASTS

| | | |
|---|---|---|
| 220 calories | 70 mg cholesterol | 1 g fiber |
| 9 g fat | 277 mg sodium | 27 g protein |
| 1 g saturated fat | 6 g carbohydrate | 437 mg potassium |

# CHICKEN RICE PILAF

*Ginger, cardamom, and saffron lend their rich flavors to this highly aromatic chicken and rice dish. Add a vegetable or salad and you have a very impressive, complete meal.*

## INGREDIENTS

1 recipe Pepper Chicken (page 205)

2 tablespoons butter or oil

3 (½-inch each) slivers cinnamon stick

1 bay leaf

½ cup onion slices (sliced lengthwise) plus ¼ cup for garnish (optional)

1 cup basmati rice

¼ teaspoon ground turmeric

2 whole cloves

1 teaspoon ground cardamom

1 tablespoon grated fresh ginger

3 threads saffron (optional)

¼ teaspoon salt (more or less to taste)

2 cups hot water

¼ cup chopped fresh cilantro

¼ cup toasted cashew pieces

1 hard-cooked egg, dusted with ¼ teaspoon of black pepper and some ground cumin (optional)

Yield: 6 cups
Serving size: 1 cup

1. Prepare Pepper Chicken and reserve, keeping warm. Preheat oven to 350°F.

2. Heat butter or oil in a large nonstick, wide-bottomed saucepan over medium heat. Add cinnamon slivers, bay leaf, onion slices, and rice. Cook for 2 to 3 minutes while stirring, until rice becomes slightly toasted.

3. Add turmeric, cloves, cardamom, ginger, saffron (if using), salt, and hot water. Stir well and bring to a boil. Reduce to a simmer, cover, and continue cooking over low heat about 10 to 15 minutes or until all liquid is absorbed and rice is tender.

4. Add reserved Pepper Chicken and cilantro; stir to blend.

5. Transfer chicken mixture into a rectangular baking dish. Sprinkle top with cashew pieces. Cover with aluminum foil. Place in preheated oven and bake for about 20 minutes.

6. Garnish with onion slices and hard-cooked egg, if using, and serve.

## NUTRITION PER SERVING USING CHICKEN THIGHS

| | | |
|---|---|---|
| 297 calories | 55 mg cholesterol | 1 g fiber |
| 17 g fat | 403 mg sodium | 18 g protein |
| 5 g saturated fat | 19 g carbohydrate | 219 mg potassium |

## NUTRITION PER SERVING USING CHICKEN BREASTS

| | | |
|---|---|---|
| 270 calories | 55 mg cholesterol | 1 g fiber |
| 12 g fat | 350 mg sodium | 20 g protein |
| 3.5 g saturated fat | 19 g carbohydrate | 342 mg potassium |

# SPICE-RUBBED OVEN-ROASTED CHICKEN

*Roasting whole spices is one of the best methods of drawing out their rich flavors. You'll see what a difference it makes. In this recipe, spice-rubbed chicken becomes extra tender and flavorful as it slowly roasts in the oven. You can also use chicken breasts, turkey breast, or Cornish hens in this recipe.*

## INGREDIENTS

5 skinless chicken thighs (about 1½ pounds)

### SPICE PASTE

¼ cup yellow or green split peas

1 tablespoon black peppercorns

1 tablespoon cumin seeds

2 whole dried red chili peppers (more or less to taste)

2 teaspoons whole coriander seeds

½ teaspoon salt (more or less to taste)

½ teaspoon turmeric

2 teaspoons finely minced garlic

¼ cup oil

Yield: 5 thighs

Serving size: 1 thigh

1. Wipe chicken with a damp paper towel and set aside.

2. Place split peas, peppercorns, cumin seeds, red chili peppers, and coriander seeds in a small, heavy skillet over medium-high heat. Toast, stirring constantly, about 2 to 5 minutes, until the spices start to look toasted and emit a wonderful aroma. Immediately place spices in a shallow bowl and let cool for 5 minutes.

3. Put cooled spices in a spice/coffee grinder and grind until coarse. Place spice mixture in a bowl, add salt, turmeric, garlic, and oil; stir to form a paste.

4. Rub chicken with spice paste. Cover and refrigerate for 20 to 30 minutes. Preheat oven to 350°F.

5. Arrange chicken on foil-covered baking pan. Roast about 25 minutes until chicken is tender and internal temperature has reached 165°F.

## NUTRITION PER SERVING

| | | |
|---|---|---|
| 360 calories | 150 mg cholesterol | 1 g fiber |
| 19 g fat | 389 mg sodium | 39 g protein |
| 3.5 g saturated fat | 8 g carbohydrate | 463 mg potassium |

# GROUND TURKEY WITH LENTILS AND COCONUT

*Delicately seasoned turkey makes a wonderful side dish, but you can also use this mixture in corn tortillas as a "taco-style" filling and add your favorite toppings.*

Yield: 3 cups

Serving size: ½ cup

## INGREDIENTS

2 cups water

¾ teaspoon ground turmeric (divided)

½ cup dry yellow or green split peas

1 tablespoon oil

1 bay leaf

2 (½-inch each) slivers cinnamon sticks

½ teaspoon cumin seeds

½ teaspoon fennel seeds

½ cup chopped onion

3 cloves garlic, finely chopped

1 fresh green chili pepper, chopped (more or less to taste)

½ pound ground turkey

½ teaspoon garam masala

½ teaspoon ground cumin

¼ teaspoon salt (more or less to taste)

2 tablespoons grated fresh coconut or unsweetened shredded dried coconut

1 tablespoon chopped cilantro

1. Bring 2 cups water and ¼ teaspoon turmeric to a boil in a 1-quart saucepan. Add split peas, reduce heat to medium and cook, uncovered, for about 20 minutes, until split peas soften and lose their shape. If water evaporates during the cooking process, add ½ cup more. Drain and reserve.

2. Heat oil in a skillet over medium-high heat (the oil should be hot but not smoking). Add bay leaf, cinnamon slivers, cumin seeds, and fennel seeds. Stir about 1 minute until cumin seeds change color from light brown to semi-dark brown.

3. Add onion, garlic, chili pepper, and remaining ½ teaspoon turmeric. Cook for 1 minute while stirring.

4. Add turkey. Stir and break apart with the back of a spoon until browned.

5. Add reserved split peas, garam masala, ground cumin, and salt; stir to combine. Cover and cook over medium-low heat for 2 to 3 minutes, stirring occasionally.

6. Add coconut and cilantro, stir, and serve.

## NUTRITION PER SERVING

| | | |
|---|---|---|
| 160 calories | 30 mg cholesterol | 1 g fiber |
| 7 g fat | 150 mg sodium | 12 g protein |
| 2 g saturated fat | 14 g carbohydrate | 164 mg potassium |

# TURKEY AND QUINOA BURGERS

*These tasty turkey burgers go well with Tomato and Onion Chutney (page 57) or Spinach Yogurt Dip (page 37).*

## INGREDIENTS

½ cup cooked quinoa (page 11)

1 teaspoon oil

½ teaspoon cumin seeds

½ cup finely chopped onion

2 cloves garlic, finely chopped

1 pound ground turkey

2 teaspoons ground turmeric

1 tablespoon garam masala

¼ teaspoon salt (more or less to taste)

Yield: 6 burgers

Serving size: 1 burger

1. Prepare quinoa and Tomato and Onion Chutney or Spinach Yogurt Dip, if using, then reserve.

2. Heat oil in a skillet over medium-high heat (the oil should be hot but not smoking). Add cumin seeds and stir until seeds change color from light brown to semi-dark brown.

3. Add onion and cook about 2 to 3 minutes, while stirring, until onions become translucent. Add garlic and cook 1 minute. Transfer mixture to a bowl, then add quinoa, turkey, turmeric, garam masala, and salt; mix well.

4. Form turkey mixture into 6 burgers. Brush with oil. Heat skillet or grill pan over medium-high heat. Add burgers and cook about 3 to 5 minutes per side until golden brown. (Burgers may also be broiled if desired.)

5. Serve with Onion Tomato Chutney or Spinach Yogurt Dip if desired.

## NUTRITION PER SERVING

| | | |
|---|---|---|
| 120 calories | 30 mg cholesterol | 1 g fiber |
| 2.5 g fat | 240 mg sodium | 20 g protein |
| 0 g saturated fat | 7 g carbohydrate | 92 mg potassium |

# TURKEY MEATBALLS

*These oven-baked meatballs are easy and quick to prepare. Also try them with ground chicken or lamb.*

Yield: 14 meatballs

Serving size: 3 meatballs

## INGREDIENTS

½ pound ground turkey

¼ cup finely minced onion

1 fresh red chili pepper, finely minced

1 teaspoon minced garlic

1½ teaspoons ground turmeric

1½ teaspoons garam masala

¼ teaspoon salt (more or less to taste)

¼ teaspoon cayenne pepper (more or less to taste)

1 tablespoon minced fresh cilantro

1. Preheat oven to 400°F.

2. Combine all ingredients in a bowl. Mix well using your hands to ensure everything is evenly distributed.

3. Take 1 tablespoon of the turkey mixture into your hands and roll into a ball. Continue until you have used all of the mixture—you should have about 14 meatballs.

4. Place meatballs on a foil-lined baking sheet. Spray the meatballs on all sides with oil or cooking spray. Bake about 10 to 12 minutes, turning balls until browned and cooked through.

## NUTRITION PER SERVING

| | | |
|---|---|---|
| 110 calories | 55 mg cholesterol | 0 g fiber |
| 6 g fat | 250 mg sodium | 12 g protein |
| 2 g saturated fat | 2 g carbohydrate | 201 mg potassium |

# EGG CURRY

*Hard-cooked eggs soak up delicate flavors when simmered in a rich, seasoned curry sauce. You can serve this over rice or quinoa.*

## INGREDIENTS

4 eggs

1 tablespoon oil

3 (½-inch each) slivers cinnamon stick

¼ teaspoon fenugreek seeds (optional)

¼ teaspoon cumin seeds

¼ teaspoon fennel seeds

½ cup chopped onion

¼ cup chopped tomato

4 cloves garlic, quartered

¼ teaspoon ground turmeric

1 cup no-salt-added tomato sauce

1 cup warm water

1 teaspoon curry powder

½ teaspoon cayenne pepper (more or less to taste)

½ teaspoon Black Pepper Cumin Powder (page 9)

¼ teaspoon salt (more or less to taste)

2 tablespoons minced fresh cilantro

Yield: 4 eggs and 2 cups sauce

Serving size: 1 egg with ½ cup sauce

1. Place eggs in a small saucepan and cover with cold water. Heat almost to a boil; remove from heat, cover and let stand for 20 minutes. Drain. Add ice water and let cool. Peel and reserve.

2. Heat oil in a skillet over medium-high heat (the oil should be hot but not smoking). Add cinnamon slivers, fenugreek seeds (if using), cumin seeds, and fennel seeds. Stir about 1 minute until cumin seeds change color from light brown to semi-dark brown.

3. Add onion, tomato, garlic, and turmeric. Cook for 1 minute while stirring.

4. Add tomato sauce, warm water, curry powder, cayenne pepper, Black Pepper Cumin Powder, and salt; stir to combine. Bring to a boil. Reduce heat to medium-low and simmer about 2 minutes, stirring occasionally.

5. Score eggs on each end with tip of a knife and add to the simmering sauce, spooning sauce over the eggs. Let stand about 10 minutes before serving so eggs can absorb the flavor of the sauce.

6. Serve garnished with minced cilantro.

## NUTRITION PER SERVING

| | | |
|---|---|---|
| 140 calories | 215 mg cholesterol | 2 g fiber |
| 8 g fat | 220 mg sodium | 7 g protein |
| 2 g saturated fat | 9 g carbohydrate | 94 mg potassium |

# LAMB STEW

*There is nothing heartier than a lamb stew, and this one, with its rich ginger-garlic sauce, makes for a delicious, satisfying meal. Serve over rice, quinoa, or polenta.*

Yield: 3 cups

Serving size: 1 cup

## INGREDIENTS

1 pound lamb

2 tablespoons oil

3 (½-inch each) slivers cinnamon stick

½ teaspoon cumin seeds

½ teaspoon fennel seeds

½ cup chopped onion

½ cup chopped tomato

3 cloves garlic, quartered

1 tablespoon grated fresh ginger

½ teaspoon ground turmeric

2 teaspoons curry powder

½ teaspoon Black Pepper Cumin Powder (page 9)

½ teaspoon cayenne pepper (more or less to taste)

½ cup no-salt-added tomato sauce

2 cups warm water

½ teaspoon salt (more or less to taste)

¼ cup chopped fresh cilantro

1. Cut lamb into cubes (you should have about 2 cups). Remove fat. Wipe the meat with a paper towel and reserve.

2. Heat oil in a skillet over medium-high heat (the oil should be hot but not smoking). Add cinnamon slivers, cumin seeds, and fennel seeds. Stir until cumin seeds change color from light brown to semi-dark brown.

3. Add onion, tomato, garlic, ginger, and turmeric. Cook and stir for 2 to 3 minutes until onions are tender.

4. Add reserved lamb; cook and stir about 3 to 5 minutes until lamb begins to turn pink. Add curry powder, Black Pepper Cumin Powder, and cayenne pepper; stir to combine.

5. Add tomato sauce, warm water, salt, and cilantro and bring to a boil. Reduce heat to medium-low, cover, and simmer about 30 minutes, stirring occasionally and adding ¼ cup of water at a time, if needed, until lamb is tender and sauce thickens.

### VARIATION:

**Saag Lamb Stew** can be prepared by adding 1 package fresh baby spinach (6 to 10 ounces) to the stew and cooking until tender.

## NUTRITION PER SERVING

| | | |
|---|---|---|
| 350 calories | 95 mg cholesterol | 2 g fiber |
| 19 g fat | 330 mg sodium | 32 g protein |
| 4.5 g saturated fat | 10 g carbohydrate | 822 mg potassium |

# DESSERTS

# ALMOND MILK WITH CARDAMOM AND FRUIT

*Drink the lightly sweetened milk and eat the fruit with a spoon. Two treats in one!*

## INGREDIENTS

⅓ cup sliced or slivered almonds

2 cups unsweetened almond milk (or any milk you prefer)

1 tablespoon honey*

½ teaspoon ground cardamom

Pinch saffron (optional)

¾ cup cut-up fresh fruit (such as mango, papaya, apricot, pineapple, or canned tropical fruit in light syrup)

———————

*If you prefer a sweeter taste, add more honey or stevia herbal sweetener.

Yield: 3 cups

Serving size: 1 cup

1. Place almonds and almond milk in a blender; blend about 3 minutes or until smooth.

2. Heat and stir almond milk mixture in a saucepan over medium heat until it comes to a boil.

3. Remove from heat; stir in honey, cardamom, saffron (if using), and fruit. Refrigerate until time to serve.

4. Serve garnished with fresh berries and pistachios if desired.

## NUTRITION PER SERVING

| | | |
|---|---|---|
| 180 calories | 0 mg cholesterol | 3 g fiber |
| 10 g fat | 100 mg sodium | 4 g protein |
| 0.5 g saturated fat | 20 g carbohydrate | 293 mg potassium |

# BROILED MANGO

*The beauty of this dish is its utter simplicity—only three ingredients, but they come together in a delectable way. Broiling brings out the sweetness of the mango, which contrasts nicely with the lime. The cardamom adds just the right seasoning.*

## INGREDIENTS

1 mango

Fresh lime

Pinch of cardamom

Yield: 1⅓ cups

Serving size: ⅓ cup

1. Position rack in upper third of oven and preheat broiler to 500°F.

2. Peel and slice mango. Arrange mango slices in a single layer on a broiler pan covered with foil.

3. Broil 8 to 10 minutes until browned in spots.

4. Squeeze lime juice over the broiled mango. Sprinkle with ground cardamom.

## NUTRITION PER SERVING

| | | |
|---|---|---|
| 140 calories | 0 mg cholesterol | 4 g fiber |
| 0 g fat | 0 g sodium | 1 g protein |
| 0 g saturated fat | 35 g carbohydrate | 342 mg potassium |

# CARROT HALWA

*This delectable halwa is fit for a king! The rich flavors of butter, almond, cardamom, saffron, and orange extract make it irresistible. Try eating just one serving!*

Yield: 1½ cups

Serving size: ¼ cup

### INGREDIENTS

1 tablespoon chopped walnuts

1 cup unsweetened almond milk

1 tablespoon butter

2 cups grated carrots

4 threads saffron (optional)

2 tablespoons brown sugar or honey

½ teaspoon ground cardamom

¼ teaspoon orange extract

¼ cup raisins, chopped

1 tablespoon pistachios (optional)

1. Toast walnuts in dry skillet until golden. Microwave milk for 2 minutes. Reserve.

2. Melt butter in a heavy-bottomed saucepan over medium heat. Add carrots and cook, stirring, for 3 to 5 minutes.

3. Add reserved hot milk and saffron (if using). When the milk comes to a boil, reduce heat to medium-low and cook about 15 minutes, stirring, until milk is absorbed.

4. Add brown sugar or honey and continue to cook carrots over medium-low heat, stirring, until carrots soften and mixture thickens. Add cardamom, orange extract, and raisins. Mix well.

5. Scoop halwa into a dish and garnish with pistachios, if desired. Serve at room temperature or chilled.

### VARIATION:

Substitute ready to serve tapioca pudding for the almond milk for a thicker creamier version.

## NUTRITION PER SERVING

| | | |
|---|---|---|
| 60 calories | 5 mg cholesterol | 2 g fiber |
| 1.5 g fat | 1 g protein | 50 mg sodium |
| 0 g saturated fat | 12 g carbohydrate | 199 mg potassium |

# MANGO LASSI

*Ah, the mango lassi—a beloved drink in India! Serve chilled as a refreshing hot weather drink.*

## INGREDIENTS

1 cup mango pulp (can be prepared from fresh, ripe mango pureed in a food processor or purchased canned)

1 cup low-fat cultured buttermilk *

1 tablespoon honey

Few drops rose essence** (optional)

Chopped pistachios (optional)

---

\* You can replace buttermilk with unsweetened vanilla almond milk.

\*\* Rose essence is used throughout India and the Middle East for sweets. You should be able to find rosewater at Indian or Middle Eastern grocers.

Yield: 2 cups

Serving size: 1 cup

1. Combine mango pulp, buttermilk, honey, and rose essence, if using.
2. Pour over ice in two tall glasses and top with pistachios if desired.

### VARIATION:

For a **Rum Mango Lassi**, add 2 tablespoons rum to each glass, stir and serve.

## NUTRITION PER SERVING

| | | |
|---|---|---|
| 170 calories | 10 mg cholesterol | 1 g fiber |
| 3 g fat | 6 g protein | 110 mg sodium |
| 1.5 g saturated fat | 34 g carbohydrate | 402 mg potassium |

# POACHED PEARS WITH GINGER AND CARDAMOM

*Pears flavored with ginger, cardamom, cinnamon, and cloves, then drizzled with a sweet syrup contrast with the tart crunch of pomegranate seeds in this aromatic treat.*

## INGREDIENTS

2 cups apple or pear juice

2 tablespoons honey

2 teaspoons grated fresh ginger

½ teaspoon ground cardamom

2 cinnamon sticks

4 whole cloves

Peel of half a lemon (colored part only, no white)

3 semi-ripe Anjou pears, rinsed

3 tablespoons pomegranate seeds or sliced almonds

Yield: 6 pear halves

Serving size: 1 pear half

1. Combine apple or pear juice, honey, ginger, cardamom, cinnamon sticks, cloves, and lemon peel in a wide-bottomed saucepan; bring to a simmer.

2. Meanwhile, peel pears, halve lengthwise, and use a teaspoon to scoop out the core. Place the pear halves cut-side down in the saucepan and simmer for 5 minutes. Turn over and simmer for another 5 minutes. They should be slightly firm. With a slotted spoon, carefully lift each pear half out of the liquid and place on plates.

3. Remove cinnamon sticks and cloves. Bring the liquid to a boil and continue to boil until it reduces by half and thickens slightly.

4. Drizzle 1 tablespoon of the reduced liquid over each pear half just before serving. Garnish with pomegranate seeds or almonds.

5. Serve at room temperature or refrigerate and serve chilled. Add a spoonful of Greek yogurt, if desired.

## NUTRITION PER SERVING

| | | |
|---|---|---|
| 130 calories | 0 mg cholesterol | 4 g fiber |
| 0 g fat | 0 mg sodium | 1 g protein |
| 0 g saturated fat | 34 g carbohydrate | 155 mg potassium |

# ROASTED PLUMS WITH SPICED WALNUTS

*Cool, creamy yogurt topped with roasted plums and sweet and spicy nuts makes for a tasty treat.*

## INGREDIENTS

2 tablespoons chopped walnuts

1 teaspoon oil

⅛ teaspoon ground cumin

¼ teaspoon ground cinnamon

¼ teaspoon ground dry ginger

A pinch ground cardamom

4 medium plums, pitted and cut into slices

1 cup plain unsweetened Greek yogurt or your favorite yogurt

Yield: 2 cups

Serving size: ½ cup

1. Preheat oven to 300°F.

2. Toss together walnuts, oil, cumin, cinnamon, ginger, and cardamom. Spread on a baking sheet. Bake nuts for 15 minutes. Let cool; reserve.

3. Increase heat to 400°F. Place plum slices on baking sheet and bake for 10 to 15 minutes until starting to brown on edges.

4. Divide yogurt into four dishes and top with plums and reserved nuts. Serve.

## NUTRITION PER SERVING

| | | |
|---|---|---|
| 90 calories | 5 mg cholesterol | 1 g fiber |
| 4.5 g fat | 45 mg sodium | 4 g protein |
| 1 g saturated fat | 9 g carbohydrate | 211 mg potassium |

# SWEET BLACK RICE WITH CARDAMOM AND COCONUT

*Here's an entirely new take on rice pudding—a delectable dessert made with whole-grain black rice that's slightly sweet and sticky with a hint of spice.*

## INGREDIENTS

2 cups water

1 cup black rice*

¼ cup sugar

½ teaspoon ground cardamom

¼ teaspoon ground cinnamon

1 tablespoon melted butter (ghee)

¼ cup grated fresh coconut or unsweetened shredded dried coconut

Optional garnish: pineapple, banana, papaya, or mango

---

*Black rice is a whole-grain, black-colored rice with hundreds of varieties. It is also known as "forbidden rice," Thai purple rice, Chinese black rice, Indonesian black rice, and Thai black rice. Glutinous black rice is a type of short-grained black rice that is especially sticky when cooked but does not contain gluten.

Yield: 2 cups

Serving size: ¼ cup

1. Bring 2 cups water to a boil. Add rice and cook for about 25 minutes or until soft and water is absorbed. (A pressure cooker can be used to cook rice quickly.)

2. Add sugar, cardamom, cinnamon, melted butter, and coconut to the rice. Mix well.

3. Serve at room temperature or cold. Garnish with fruit as desired.

## NUTRITION PER SERVING

| | | |
|---|---|---|
| 130 calories | 5 mg cholesterol | 2 g fiber |
| 3.5 g fat | 0 mg sodium | 2 g protein |
| 2 g saturated fat | 24 g carbohydrate | 86 mg potassium |

# SWEET MANGO SAUCE

*This sauce is an unusual sweet and savory topping for Greek yogurt or ice cream.*

### INGREDIENTS

1 cup chopped ripe mango or canned mango pulp*

⅔ cup water

1 tablespoon brown sugar

1 teaspoon grated fresh ginger

½ teaspoon oil

1 whole dried red chili pepper (more or less to taste)

¼ teaspoon black mustard seeds

_____

*Mango pulp is available in ethnic and Indian grocery stores.

Yield: 1 cup
Serving size: ¼ cup

1. In a small saucepan over medium heat, cook mango in ⅔ cup water until very soft.

2. Add brown sugar and ginger. Mix well.

3. Heat oil in a skillet over medium-high heat (the oil should be hot but not smoking). Add red chili pepper and mustard seeds and stir until mustard seeds start to pop. Remove the chili pepper and add this seasoning to the cooked mango mixture and mix well.

4. Serve over plain Greek yogurt or ice cream and sprinkle with cayenne pepper, if desired.

## NUTRITION PER SERVING

| | | |
|---|---|---|
| 35 calories | 0 mg cholesterol | 1 g fiber |
| 1 g fat | 0 mg sodium | 68 mg potassium |
| 0 g saturated fat | 8 g carbohydrate | |

# TAPIOCA PUDDING

*Delicious, creamy tapioca pudding with a hint of almond and cardamom.*

Yield: 2 cups
Serving size: ½ cup

### INGREDIENTS

2 cups unsweetened vanilla almond milk

¼ cup quick-cooking tapioca

2 tablespoons sugar

1 tablespoon stevia in the raw or honey

¼ teaspoon coconut extract or vanilla extract

¼ teaspoon ground cardamom

Fresh blueberries or diced mango (optional)

1. Combine almond milk, tapioca, and sugar in a saucepan; let stand for 5 minutes.

2. Heat milk mixture on medium heat until it comes to a boil, stirring constantly. Remove from heat, stir in stevia or honey, coconut or vanilla extract, and cardamom. Taste and add more sweetener if desired.

3. Divide into 4 dishes. Serve warm or chilled, topped with fresh berries or mango.

## NUTRITION PER SERVING

| | | |
|---|---|---|
| 70 calories | 0 mg cholesterol | 1 g fiber |
| 2 g fat | 90 mg sodium | 1 g protein |
| 0 g saturated fat | 15 g carbohydrate | 75 mg potassium |

# SUGGESTED MEAT & SEAFOOD MENUS

Spice-Rubbed Oven-Roasted Chicken *page 209*
Cauliflower Rice Pilaf *page 93*
Green Beans with Lentils and Coconut *page 147*
Carrots in Seasoned Yogurt *page 73*

❖❖

Lamb Stew *page 219*
Cabbage Rice Pilaf with Cashews *page 89*
Roasted Brussels Sprouts *page 131*
Minty Cucumber and Yogurt *page 77*

❖❖

Chicken Rice Pilaf *page 207*
Egg Curry *page 217*
*or*
A hard-cooked egg seasoned with black pepper and ground cumin
Seasoned Vegetable Yogurt Salad *page 83*
Roasted Plums with Spiced Walnuts *page 233*

❖❖

Spicy Seared Shrimp *page 197*
Black Pepper and Cumin Rice with Cashews *page 87*
Tri-colored Bell Peppers *page 119*
Almond Milk with Cardamom and Fruit *page 223*

❖❖

Fish in Ginger-Garlic Sauce *page 189*
Carrot Rice Pilaf *page 91*
Asparagus with Ginger *page 115*

❖❖

Black-Eyed Pea Soup *page 61*
Turkey and Quinoa Burgers *page 213*
Cilantro Chutney *page 45*
Roasted Vegetables *page 185*

# SUGGESTED VEGETARIAN MENUS

Black Bean Cutlets *page 21*
Peanut and Coconut Chutney *page 53*
Flavored Quinoa *page 105*
Bell Peppers in Lentil Sauce *page 121*

❖❖

Spinach Lentil Rice *page 99*
Carrots and Tomatoes in Lentil Sauce *page 137*
Roasted Potato Medley *page 161*

❖❖

Lentil Crepes *page 25*
Potatoes in Onion and Tomato Sauce *page 165*
Eggplant Chutney *page 47*

❖❖

Plain Basmati Rice *page 10*
Green Bell Peppers and Red Radishes in Lentil Sauce *page 123*
Broccoli with Red Onion and Ginger *page 125*

❖❖

Fragrant Lemon Rice *page 97*
Eggplant Curry with Green Peas *page 143*
Heavenly Lima Beans *page 149*

❖❖

Vegetable Rice Pilaf *page 103*
Seasoned Potatoes in Lentil Sauce *page 167*
Green Beans with Carrots *page 145*

# SUGGESTED FUSION MENUS

The recipes in this cookbook "fuse" beautifully with Western favorites. Use your imagination and have fun blending the dishes.

### With Grilled, Roasted, or Baked Chicken

Any 1 Flavored Rice Dish *or* Quinoa *or* Polenta, such as:

Spinach Lentil Rice *page 99*
Tomato and Green Onion Rice *page 101*
Vegetable Quinoa *page 109*
Flavorful Polenta *page 111*

1 or more Vegetable Dishes, such as:

Butternut Squash with Cilantro *page 175*
Crunchy Cabbage with Ginger and Coconut *page 135*
Sweet Potatoes with Coconut *page 169*

### With Grilled Fish or Shrimp

Any 1 Flavored Rice Dish, such as:

Black Pepper and Cumin Rice with Cashews *page 87*
Fragrant Lemon Rice *page 97*

1 or more Vegetable Dishes, such as:

Brussels Sprouts with Chickpeas *page 129*
Eggplant Curry with Green Peas *page 143*
Sweet Potatoes with Coconut *page 169*

# SUGGESTED THANKSGIVING & HOLIDAY SIDE DISHES

The following vibrant, colorful appetizers and side dishes will bring a unique blend of fusion flavors to your holiday meals. East can meet West right at your dinner table!

### Appetizers (*Select one or two items*):

Savory Tuna (with rice crackers or spread on toasted gluten-free bread) *page 35*
Spinach Yogurt Dip (with gluten-free chips) *page 37*
Eggplant Chutney (with gluten-free breads or rice crackers) *page 47*
Peanut and Coconut Chutney (served as a dip with fresh vegetables) *page 53*
Seasoned Apple Relish (served on toasted gluten-free bread) *page 55*
Carrots in Seasoned Yogurt (with chips or rice crackers) *page 73*

### Flavored Rice Dishes (*Select one item*):

Black Pepper and Cumin Rice with Cashews *page 87*
Carrot Rice Pilaf *page 91*
Cauliflower Rice Pilaf *page 93*
Fragrant Lemon Rice *page 97*
Tomato and Green Onion Rice *page 101*
Vegetable Rice Pilaf *page 103*
Vegetable Quinoa *page 109*

### Vegetable Side Dishes (*Select one or more items*):

Roasted Brussels Sprouts *page 131*
Seasoned Corn *page 141*
Green Beans with Carrots *page 145*
Green Beans with Lentils and Coconut *page 147*
Roasted Potato Medley *page 161*
Seasoned Mashed Potatoes—a sure winner! *page 163*
Sweet Potatoes with Coconut *page 169*
Roasted Vegetables *page 185*
Butternut Squash with Cilantro *page 175*

# INDEX

# ABOUT THE AUTHORS

ALAMELU VAIRAVAN is host of Healthful Indian Flavors with Alamelu on public television. She is also a culinary educator and author of several cookbooks, including *Healthy South Indian Cooking, Expanded Edition* (Hippocrene Books, 2008). Alamelu holds a degree in Health Information Management from the University of Wisconsin-Milwaukee. She maintains a residence in Wisconsin and Arizona. Visit her at curryonwheels.com.

MARGARET PFEIFFER, MS, RD, CLS, is a practicing cardiac nutritionist, a clinical lipid specialist and registered dietitian. She is also the author of *Smart 4 Your Heart* (King, 2009). She resides in Brookfield, Wisconsin.

# Also by Alamelu Vairavan . . .

## HEALTHY SOUTH INDIAN COOKING
### Expanded Edition
*Alamelu Vairavan and Dr. Patricia Marquardt*

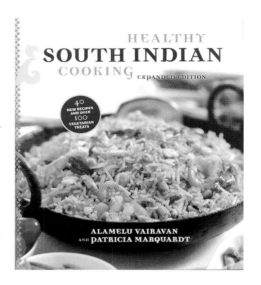

*"Coconut-infused curries, brilliant vegetable dishes . . . what could be complex becomes relatively simple in Vairavan's approach . . ."*
—Los Angeles Times

*"Besides 100 feast-worthy vegetarian recipes, [the authors] explain how the spices that make Indian cuisine so fragrant and flavorful also pack a whallop of nutrients and disease-fighting phytochemicals."*
—Wisconsin State Journal

*"Dals, chutneys and curries take their place along with fare that might be totally new to many . . . the authors do a remarkably good job of keeping the recipes relatively simple and accessible."*

—The Post-Crescent

In the famous Chettinad cooking tradition of southern India, these mostly vegetarian recipes allow home cooks to create dishes such as Potato-filled Dosas with Coconut Chutney; Pearl Onion and Tomato Sambhar; Chickpea and Bell Pepper Poriyal; and Eggplant Masala Curry. *Rasams*, breads, legumes and *payasams* are all featured here, as is the exceptional Chettinad Chicken Kolambu, South India's version of the popular *vindaloo*. Each of these low-fat, low-calorie recipes come with a complete nutritional analysis. Also included are sample menus and innovative suggestions for integrating South Indian dishes into traditional Western meals. A section on the varieties and methods of preparation for *dals* (a lentil dish that is a staple of this cuisine), a multilingual glossary of spices and ingredients, and 16 pages of color photographs make this book a clear and concise introduction to the healthy, delicious cooking of South India.

ISBN: 0-7818-1189-9 · $35.00hc